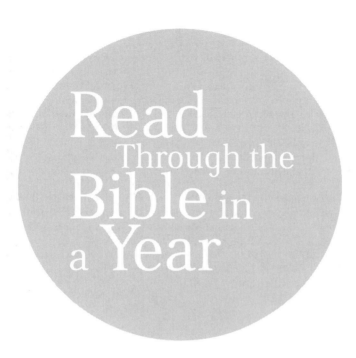

Read Through the Bible in a Year

John R. Kohlenberger III

MOODY PUBLISHERS
CHICAGO

All Scripture quotations, unless otherwise indicated, are taken from the *Holy Bible, New International Version*®. NIV®. Copyright © 1973, 1978, 1984 by International Bible Society. Used by permission of Zondervan Publishing House. All rights reserved. Scripture quotations marked KJV are taken from the King James Version.

Scripture quotations marked NASB are taken from the *New American Standard Bible*®, Copyright © 1960, 1962, 1963, 1968, 1971, 1972, 1973, 1975, 1977, 1995 by The Lockman Foundation. Used by permission. (www.Lockman.org)

Material in "Vital Information: Background" in each chapter first appeared in the Ryrie Study Bible, Expanded Edition (Chicago: Moody, 1994), and is used by permission.

Several articles first appeared in Howard G. Hendricks and William D. Hendricks, *Living by the Book* (Chicago: Moody, 2007) and are used by permission (verbatim except as noted): "First Things First," pp. 21–25, (adapted); "Ten Strategies for First-Rate Reading" Part 1," 79–80, 83–84, 89–90; Part 2, 94–98 (adapted); 100, 106–107 (adapted); Part 3: 114–15, 118, 119, 127–32, 134 (adapted); "A Proven Method for Studying the Bible," 39–40, 44; "What Type of Literature Is This?" Part 1, 213–22; "Prophecy and Apocalyptic Literature," 222–23.

Editor: Jim Vincent
Inside Design: Smartt Guys design
Cover Design: Paetzold Design
Cover Image: Getty Images

Library of Congress Cataloging-in-Publication Data

Kohlenberger, John R.
  Read through the Bible in a year / John R. Kohlenberger III.
    p. cm.
  ISBN 978-0-8024-7167-3
  1. Bible—Reading. 2. Bible—Criticism, interpretation, etc. I. Title.
  BS617.K63 2008
  220.6'1--dc22

                                                            2008026981

We hope you enjoy this book from Moody Publishers. Our goal is to provide high-quality, thought-provoking books and products that connect truth to your real needs and challenges. For more information on other books and products written and produced from a biblical perspective, go to www.moodypublishers.com or write to:

Moody Publishers
820 N. LaSalle Boulevard
Chicago, IL 60610

3 5 7 9 10 8 6 4 2

Printed in the United States of America

Contents

Welcome

For some of you, this may be your first try at successfully reading through the entire Bible. For others, you've tried before with slight success. I have a hunch that most Christians who attempt to read through the Bible never complete it, not because they are unspiritual or uncommitted, but because it is a difficult task.

One difficulty comes when a reading program bounces back and forth between the Old and New Testaments, interrupting the flow and continuity of the books. Another unnecessary difficulty comes in using a translation that does not communicate in a language you readily understand. But even reading one book at a time in biblical order is difficult because of the parallels and overlaps of certain books. The four Gospels, for example, present the life of Christ, but no two have exactly the same order or relate precisely the same events.

To try to overcome that disorientation, this read-through-the-Bible booklet is arranged in a general chronological order. As much as possible, we will read whole books at a time. But we will read Samuel, Kings, and Chronicles together, with Psalms, Proverbs, the prophets, and other texts appropriately inserted. We will also read the Gospels as one account and the letters of Paul within the framework of Acts.

This format, however, will not simply serve as a history lesson. We will concentrate on the most important subject in the Bible—God Himself. Because we will read the Bible in historical order, we will have an opportunity to see how God has progressively revealed Himself in word and action.

As you make your way through this book, you'll find a variety of resources that can help you maintain focus and momentum throughout the year. Each month divides these resources into two distinct types. The "Getting to Know You" sections are designed to bring you deeper into the mystery and power of the Scriptures. Here you will find information about the historical context of biblical authors and material, as well as in-depth explorations of key words, names, and phrases. You'll also find a helpful overview of each of the Bible's sixty-six books.

The "Going Deeper" sections that conclude each month have been designed primarily to motivate and inspire you. They introduce you to helpful articles that will help you understand how to study the Bible properly, why God's Word can be trusted, and much more. These articles are from *Living by the Book*, a classic book on reading and knowing the holy Scriptures that is written by Howard and Bill Hendricks. My thanks to the Hendricks for their contribution to this book.

—John R. Kohlenberger III

First Things First

If you've committed to reading the Bible all the way through in one year—or even if you're just dipping your toes in the water by reading this book, trying to figure out if it's warm enough to jump—chances are good that you've had some prior experiences with God's Word. And that's a wonderful thing.

But the chances are equally good that you're not completely satisfied with those experiences. Maybe you don't understand a lot of what you read in the Bible. Maybe it's been difficult for you to find time to study it regularly, let alone every day. Or maybe reading the Bible hasn't "worked" for you yet—you don't have the relationship with God that you'd like to have, or you've been unable to gain victory over a specific area of weakness.

If so, then I have some good news and bad news for you. First the bad news: Reading the Bible is hard work. At least, reading the Bible properly is hard work. It just is.

Now the good news: Reading the Bible is hard work, but it's worth the effort. You really can achieve a meaningful, productive quiet time with God every day. You can understand what you read in the Bible, and you can learn how to apply it to your life in a way that produces spiritual growth.

It takes hard work, and it takes discipline and perseverance—but it can happen.

And the rewards are great. Invest your time in the Bible and there is a payoff.

"What difference will reading the Bible make in my life?" you ask. Here are three benefits you can expect when you invest in a study of God's Word. These benefits are truly remarkable because they are available nowhere else. And frankly, they're not luxuries, but necessities. Let's look at three passages that conspire to build a convincing case for why we must study the Bible.

SPENDING TIME IN THE BIBLE CONTRIBUTES TO GROWTH

The first passage is found in 1 Peter 2:2: "Like newborn babies, long for the pure milk of the word, so that by it you may grow in respect to salvation" (NASB).

Let me give you three words to unpack the truth contained here. Write them in the margin of your Bible, next to this verse. The first one is *attitude*. Peter is describing the attitude of a newborn baby. Just as the baby grabs for the bottle, so you grab for the Book. The baby has to have milk to sustain its life physically; you have to have the Scriptures to sustain your life spiritually.

Notice what Peter says about your appetite for the Word. You should "long" for it, he says. That's the second word: *long*. You're to crave the spiritual milk of God's Word. Now, to be honest, that's a cultivated taste. Psalm 19:10 says that Scripture is sweeter than honey, but you'd never know that judging by some believers.

You see, there are three basic kinds of Bible students. First, there is the "nasty medicine" type. To them the Word is bitter—yeeh!—but it's good for what ails them. Then there is the "shredded wheat" kind. To them Scripture is nourishing, but dry. It's like eating a bale of hay. But the third kind is what I call the "strawberries and cream" folks. They just can't get enough of the stuff. How did they acquire that taste? By feasting on the Word. They've cultivated what Peter describes here—an insatiable appetite for spiritual truth. Which of these three types are you?

There's a purpose to all of this, which brings us to the third word: *aim*. What is the aim of the Bible? The text tells us: in order that you might grow. Please note—it is not only that you may know. Certainly you can't grow without knowing. But you can know and not grow. The Bible was written not to satisfy your curiosity, but to help you conform to Christ's image. Not to make you a smarter sinner, but to make you like the Savior. Not to fill your head with a collection of biblical facts, but to transform your life.

What about you? How long have you been a Christian? Nine months? Seven or eight years? Thirty-nine years? The real issue isn't how long, but how much have you grown? Step up to God's growth chart and measure your progress. That's what this passage is teaching.

So the first reason for reading and studying Scripture is that it is a means of spiritual growth. It is God's primary tool to develop you as an individual in His kingdom.

SPENDING TIME IN THE BIBLE
CONTRIBUTES TO SPIRITUAL MATURITY

The second passage we need to look at is Hebrews 5:11-14: "Concerning him we have much to say, and it is hard to explain, since you have become dull of hearing. For though by this time you ought to be teachers, you have need again for someone to teach you the elementary principles of the oracles of God, and you have come to need milk and not solid food. For everyone who partakes only of milk is not accustomed to the word of righteousness, for he is an infant. But solid food is for the mature, who because of practice have their senses trained to discern good and evil" (NASB).

This is an instructive passage in terms of studying Scripture. The writer says he's got a lot to say, but it is "hard to explain." Why? Is it the difficulty of the revelation? No, it's the density of the reception. There's a "learning disability," Peter says. "You have become dull of hearing," meaning you are slow to learn.

The key word in this passage is *dull*. Underline it in your Bible. The writer tells his readers that, by virtue of the passing of time, they ought to be entering college. But instead they've got to go back to kindergarten and learn their ABC's all over again. "When you should be communicating the truth to others as teachers, you need to have someone communicate the truth to you," he writes.

In fact, he says, you still need milk, not solid food. Solid food is for the mature. Who are the mature? Are they the people who go to seminary? Who can whip anyone in a theological duel? Who know the most Bible verses? No, the writer says you are mature if you've trained yourself through constant use of Scripture to distinguish good from evil. The mark of spiritual maturity is not how much you understand, but how much you use. In the spiritual realm, the opposite of ignorance is not knowledge—it's obedience.

So that is a second reason Bible reading and study is essential. The Bible is the divine means of developing spiritual maturity. There is no other way.

SPENDING TIME IN THE BIBLE CONTRIBUTES TO SPIRITUAL EFFECTIVENESS

There's a third passage, 2 Timothy 3:16–17: "All Scripture is inspired by God and profitable for teaching, for reproof, for correction, for training in righteousness; so that the man of God may be adequate, equipped for every good work" (NASB).

"All Scripture," the text says. That includes 2 Chronicles. How about Deuteronomy? Can you even find it? Have you ever had your devotions in it? When Jesus was tempted in the wilderness (Matthew 4:1–11), He defeated the Devil three times by saying, "It is written." All three responses are quotations from the book of Deuteronomy. I've often thought, *If my spiritual life depended on my knowledge of Deuteronomy, how would I make out?*

Paul says all Scripture is profitable. But profitable for what? He mentions four things. First, for doctrine, or teaching. That is, it will structure your thinking. That's crucial, because if you are not thinking correctly, you are not living correctly. What you believe will determine how you behave.

He also says the Bible is profitable for rebuke. That is, it will tell you where you are out of bounds. It's like an umpire who cries, "Out!" or, "Safe!" It tells you what is sin. It tells you what God wants for your life.

Third, it is profitable for correction. Do you have a closet where you put all the junk you can't find room for anywhere else? You cram it in, and then one day you forget and open the door and—whoosh!—it all comes out. You say, "Good night, I'd better clean this thing up." The Bible is like that. It opens up the doors in your life and provides a purifying dynamic to help you clean out sin and learn to conform to God's will.

A fourth advantage of the Bible is that it is profitable for training in righteous living. God uses it to show you how to live. Having corrected you on the negatives, He gives you positive guidelines to follow as you go through life.

So what is the overall purpose of reading God's Word? In order that you might be equipped for every good work. Have you ever said, "I wish my life were more effective for Jesus Christ"? If so, what have you done to prepare yourself? Bible study is a primary means to becoming an effective servant of Jesus Christ.

One time I asked a group of businessmen, "If you didn't know any more about your business or profession than you know about Christianity after the same number of years of exposure, what would happen?"

One guy blurted out, "They'd fire me."

I said, "Thank you, sir, for the honesty."

He was right, you know. The reason God can't use you more than He wants to may well be that you are not prepared.

God asks you to come and study that Book for three compelling reasons: It's essential to growth. It's essential to maturity. It's essential for equipping you, training you, so that you might be an available, clean, sharp instrument in His hands to accomplish His purposes.

So the real question confronting you now is: How can you afford not to be in God's Word?

January

In the beginning God created the heavens and the earth.
—Genesis 1:1

BIBLE READING SCHEDULE

DATE	TEXT		DATE	TEXT
Jan 1	Gen. 1–3		Jan. 17	Gen. 41–42
Jan 2	Gen. 4:1–6:8		Jan. 18	Gen. 43–45
Jan. 3	Gen. 6:9–9:29		Jan. 19	Gen. 46–47
Jan. 4	Gen. 10–11		Jan. 20	Gen. 48–50
Jan. 5	Gen. 12–14		Jan. 21	Job 1–3
Jan. 6	Gen. 15–17		Jan. 22	Job 4–7
Jan. 7	Gen. 18–19		Jan. 23	Job 8–11
Jan. 8	Gen. 20–22		Jan. 24	Job 12–15
Jan. 9	Gen. 23–24		Jan. 25	Job 16–19
Jan. 10	Gen. 25–26		Jan. 26	Job 20–22
Jan. 11	Gen. 27–28		Jan. 27	Job 23–28
Jan. 12	Gen. 29–30		Jan. 28	Job 29–31
Jan. 13	Gen. 31–32		Jan. 29	Job 32–34
Jan. 14	Gen. 33–35		Jan. 30	Job 35–37
Jan. 15	Gen. 36–37		Jan. 31	Job 38–42
Jan. 16	Gen. 38–40			

Getting to Know . . .

GENESIS

Author: Moses

Date: 1450–1410 B.C.

Theme: Genesis is a real-life history of individual people, a fact that is emphasized by the ten sections within it that usually begin, "These are the records of the generations of . . . " (NASB). This thrust provides a natural unity to the book. Genesis is a book about the beginning of many things: the world, man, sin, civilization, the nations, and Israel. Genesis also contains important theological themes, including the doctrine of the living, personal God; the doctrine of man made in the image of God, then of sinful man; the anticipation of a Redeemer; and the covenant promises made to the nation of Israel.

Overview: Genesis takes us from creation to the settling of Jacob's descendants in Egypt; although three-fourths of the book concentrates on the four generations from the call of Abraham to the death of Joseph (2091–1805 B.C.).

The names of God vary in Genesis. God is called "the Mighty One" when He creates the universe, but it is *Yahweh* who personally forms Adam and Eve, enjoys fellowship with them in the garden, and even provides for them after their sin (Genesis 2–3). Note, too, that Melchizedek worships God Most High (*El Elyon*), but that Abram, who has a special covenant relationship with God, knows Him more intimately as *Yahweh God Most High* (14:18–24).

Several such compound names or titles give us additional insight into God's attributes and actions. Besides *El Elyon*, the most famous is *El Shaddai*, "God Almighty," although this name occurs only 48 times in the Bible. (See "Going Deeper" for more on the names of God in the Old Testament.)

JOB

Author: Uncertain. Suggestions include Job himself, Elihu, Moses, and Solomon.

Date: Uncertain.

Theme: The book wrestles with the age-old question: If God is a God of love and mercy, why do the righteous suffer? In answer, Job clearly teaches the sovereignty of God and the need for man to acknowledge that sovereignty. Job's three friends gave essentially the same answer to the problem of pain: All suffering is due to sin. Elihu, however, declared that suffering is often the means of purifying the righteous. God's purpose, therefore, was to strip away all of Job's self-righteousness, and to bring him to the place of complete trust in Him.

Overview: Though we do not know who wrote the book or when it was written, the book of Job appears to be set in the days of the patriarchs—though not in the land of Israel.

There are two keys to reading this book. One is recognizing that it is "wisdom literature"; the other is noticing the uses of the names of God. As wisdom literature, the Book of Job tells us in proverb form about the order of the world God has created. That account can be summarized in proverbs because God is a God of order. There are exceptions, however, to many proverbs because sin has marred the perfection of God's creation.

When Job's friends discover he is destitute and diseased, they immediately confront him with wisdom based on common sense: God judges the wicked and prospers the righteous, so confess your wickedness and be restored. Job, however, maintains his righteousness in spite of their seemingly well-reasoned but misapplied statements.

This is where noticing the names of God becomes important. We, the readers, have information the biblical characters did not have—the heavenly scenes presented in chapters 1 and 2. We know that Job's condition is a result of a battle between God and Satan. Our special insight is underlined by the use of the name *Yahweh*, whereas Job and his friends, who do not have the whole picture, use various names of God to refer to Him. When God finally reveals Himself in chapters 38–42, the name *Yahweh* again dominates the text.

The story of Job teaches the limitation of wisdom. Regardless of how much theology we know—or think we know—we never have the complete picture. We must use compassion rather than condemnation when dealing with others, both believers and non-believers, or we may be in danger of "[not speaking of God] what is right" (42:7). And when we seem to be on the short end of God's promises, we must wait on God and trust in Him rather than question His character.

Going Deeper . . .

The names of God in the Old Testament are all significant. In the ancient Near East, names were given to signify one's character. To learn more about the names of God, including the names used for God in Genesis and Job, turn to "Going Deeper" at the back of the book and read the article "The Primary Names of God."

February

*Moses said to God, "Suppose I go to the Israelites and say to them,
'The God of your fathers has sent me to you,' and they ask me,
'What is his name?' Then what shall I tell them?" God said to Moses,
"I am who I am. This is what you are to say to the Israelites:
'I am has sent me to you.'"*
—Exodus 3:13–14

BIBLE READING SCHEDULE

DATE	TEXT	DATE	TEXT
Feb. 1	Exod. 1–4	**Feb. 15**	Exod. 39–40
Feb. 2	Exod. 5–8	**Feb. 16**	Lev. 1:1–5:13
Feb. 3	Exod. 9–11	**Feb. 17**	Lev. 5:14–7:38
Feb. 4	Exod. 12–13	**Feb. 18**	Lev. 8–10
Feb. 5	Exod. 14–15	**Feb. 19**	Lev. 11–12
Feb. 6	Exod. 16–18	**Feb. 20**	Lev. 13–14
Feb. 7	Exod. 19–21	**Feb. 21**	Lev. 15–17
Feb. 8	Exod. 22–24	**Feb. 22**	Lev. 18–20
Feb. 9	Exod. 25–27	**Feb. 23**	Lev. 21–23
Feb. 10	Exod. 28–29	**Feb. 24**	Lev. 24–25
Feb. 11	Exod. 30–31	**Feb. 25**	Lev. 26–27
Feb. 12	Exod. 32–34	**Feb. 26**	Num. 1–2
Feb. 13	Exod. 35–36	**Feb. 27**	Num. 3–4
Feb. 14	Exod. 37–38	**Feb. 28**	Num. 5–6

Getting to Know . . .

EXODUS

Author: Moses

Date: 1450–1410 B.C.

Theme: The theme of Exodus is the deliverance of the Israelites from Egypt, in fulfillment of the promise made by God in Genesis 15:13–14. The book records the birth of the nation of Israel, the giving of the law, and the origin of ritual worship.

Overview: Exodus begins where Genesis left off: with the relocation of Jacob and his descendants to Egypt, in fulfillment of Genesis 15:13a. But in fulfillment of Genesis 15:13b, the Israelites are soon enslaved and oppressed by the Egyptians. The rest of the book begins to fulfill Genesis 15:14, 16—the exodus from Egypt to the Promised Land. The majority of Exodus concentrates on the eighty-one years between the birth of Moses and the setting up of the tabernacle (1526–1445 B.C.).

The name *Yahweh* first appears in chapter 3. God proclaims that He has "come down"—that He is specially present on Earth to deliver His people from bondage and lead them into the bountiful land of promise. Moses is the one who first gets introduced to God in this way. That's important because of the job set before him: to lead the Israelites out of Egypt.

But before Moses will lead God's people, he wants to know His name. God tells him, "I am who I am." This combination of *Yahweh* and *Ehyeh* ("I am") implies more than God's existence; it implies His intimate presence, His readiness to save and to act for His people, and the constancy of His character. Thus, we can define *Yahweh* as "I am truly present, ready to save and to act, just as I have always been."

In chapters 5–18, Israel comes to "know" Yahweh intimately as He judges Egypt and delivers Israel (6:6–8).

The Israelites, therefore, fear Yahweh and put their trust in Him (14:30–31). Because Yahweh provided for them in the wilderness en route to Sinai, they willingly enter the covenant relationship He offers in 19:3–8.

We will say more about the law later. Now, it's enough to say that the law was given for Israel's good and provided everything they needed to know about godly living. The essence of the old covenant relationship with God is identical with that of the new covenant: "If you love me, you will obey what I command" (John 14:15; Deuteronomy 6:4–9).

Israel breaks the first two commandments when the people build the golden calf and worship it as their god (Exodus 32). Though God responds with judgment, He still reveals His character as Yahweh, the compassionate and gracious God who forgives the repentant but judges the unrepentant

(34:6–7). This compassion is one of the most important revelations about the character of Yahweh, and is repeated throughout Scripture until it culminates with the coming of Jesus in John 1:14.

Chapters 36–40 emphasize Israel's response to Yahweh's forgiveness: twenty-one times the people do "just as *Yahweh* commanded." As a result, *Yahweh* fills the tabernacle with His special presence and glory (40:34–38), a powerful indication that He accepts their attitude and action.

LEVITICUS

Author: Moses
Date: 1450–1410 B.C.
Theme: The Book of Exodus concludes with the erection of the tabernacle, which was constructed according to the pattern God gave to Moses. But how was Israel to use the tabernacle? The instructions in Leviticus answer that question, and were given to Moses during the fifty days between the setting up of the tabernacle (Exodus 40:17) and the departure of the people from Sinai (Numbers 10:12). Leviticus may be viewed in three complementary ways. First, it is a book about the holiness of God and His requirements for fellowship with Himself. Second, and connected to this idea, it is also a book that reveals the sinfulness of man. Finally, it may be viewed as a book about atonement—the provision of access to God for sinful man.
Overview: The key concept in Leviticus is holiness—being set apart for God's service and being different from the world by obeying God's commands.

Believe it or not, the sacrificial system that is set up in chapters 1–7 reveals the grace of Yahweh. He is holy, separate from His people, yet He reveals a way in which His people can become holy themselves and thus have fellowship with Him. This concept is carried through the rest of the book, as many commands are punctuated with "You shall be holy, for I am holy."

This emphasis on holiness is punctuated by an interesting string of events. The first event concerns the priesthood. It is made a holy group, within an already holy people, to serve the holy God (Leviticus 8–9). But immediately following their consecration, Nadab and Abihu despise God's holiness by offering unholy fire and incense (Leviticus 10). Yahweh then protects His holiness by destroying them with the same fire that had accepted the burnt offering only the day before (10:2; 9:24). The third event depicts Yahweh again protecting His holiness when He demands the death of the man who blasphemed His name (24:10–23).

When reading Leviticus, we should marvel at the intimacy of the use of God's names. *Yahweh* appears 311 times (proportionately more than in Exodus), and all 52 occurrences of Elohim show the personal covenant relationship of God to His people: "your God" is used 40 times, "his God" is used 8 times, and "their God" is used 4 times.

Going Deeper...

You're doing a lot of reading as you move more into the Old Testament. Are you still reading for meaning? There are several strategies you can use to open up the text and become a first-rate reader. In "Going Deeper" in the back of the book some of you will learn the strategies to engage your mind, your emotions, and your spirit in the article "Ten Strategies for First-Rate Reading: Part 1" (page 63).

March

Hear, O Israel: The Lord our God, the Lord is one. Love the Lord your God with all your heart and with all your soul and with all your strength.
—Deut. 6:4–5

BIBLE READING SCHEDULE

DATE	TEXT	DATE	TEXT
March 1	Num. 7	**March 17**	Deut. 11–13
March 2	Num. 8–10	**March 18**	Deut. 14–17
March 3	Num. 11–13	**March 19**	Deut. 18–21
March 4	Num. 14–15	**March 20**	Deut. 22–25
March 5	Num. 16–18	**March 21**	Deut. 26–28
March 6	Num. 19–21	**March 22**	Deut. 29:1–31:29
March 7	Num. 22–24	**March 23**	Deut. 31:30–34:12
March 8	Num. 25–26	**March 24**	Josh. 1–4
March 9	Num. 27–29	**March 25**	Josh. 5–8
March 10	Num. 30–31	**March 26**	Josh. 9–11
March 11	Num. 32–33	**March 27**	Josh. 12–14
March 12	Num. 34–36	**March 28**	Josh. 15–17
March 13	Deut. 1–2	**March 29**	Josh. 18–19
March 14	Deut. 3–4	**March 30**	Josh. 20–22
March 15	Deut. 5–7	**March 31**	Josh. 23–Judges 1
March 16	Deut. 8–10		

Getting to Know . . .

NUMBERS

Author: Moses

Date: 1450–1410 B.C. The account covers the period between Israel's departure from Egypt and her arrival in Canaan, including the winding, thirty-nine years' journey from Sinai to Kadesh Barnea, through various places in the wilderness, and finally to the plains of Moab across the Jordan River from Jericho.

Theme: The principal lesson is that God's people must walk by faith, trusting His promises, if they are to move forward. To reinforce this theme, the book recounts the unbelief and discontent of the people in general (11:1) and of Miriam and Aaron (12:1), and the people's refusal at Kadesh Barnea to enter the Promised Land (14:2).

Overview: Numbers is characterized by the Israelites' rebellion. The justice and judgment of Yahweh is a key revelation of the book. Israel's failure to obey Yahweh is emphasized in the distinction of Numbers. In the four centuries from Jacob to the Exodus, the number of men alone grew from 70 to 625,550. But in the four decades in the desert, that number dropped to 624,730.

But Yahweh did not limit His actions to judgment during that time; He also acted in salvation. Every judgment dealt only with the core of the rebellion; the majority of the people were not destroyed. The only judgment that affected all Israel was the forty years of wandering and death in the wilderness. But even here the nation survived, and a new generation stood ready to enter the land. Furthermore, Yahweh led His people to victories over Arad, Heshbon, and Bashan (chapter 21), turned Balaam's curse into a blessing (22–24), and gave Israel vengeance against the Midianites (31).

God's presence to judge and to save is emphasized again by the dominance of the name Yahweh. Most of the other names and titles are found in Balaam's oracles.

DEUTERONOMY

Author: Moses

Date: 1410 B.C. Deuteronomy contains the addresses that Moses gave during the final months of his life, when the Israelites were encamped in the plains of Moab prior to their entrance into the Promised Land.

Theme: Being reminded of God's power can sustain His people as they face their fears of the unknown and unexpected. The people were facing war, temptation, and a new, settled way of life—all under the unproven leadership of Joshua. The congregation living after forty years of wandering had not personally experienced the deliverance at the Red Sea or the giving of the law at Sinai. They needed to be reminded of God's power and God's laws.

Overview: Theologically, Deuteronomy is one of the most important books in the Bible. It explains the dynamic relationship between Yahweh and His covenant people: He loves them and acts on their behalf, so they must love and obey Him. It contains proportionately more occurrences of the name *Yahweh* (especially "*Yahweh* your God") than any other Old Testament book. It was also the book most quoted by Jesus.

The heart of the law is expressed in several passages in Deuteronomy, though chapter 6 is certainly the best known. As Jesus repeated fourteen centuries later: "If you love me, you will obey what I command" (John 14:15). "Love" in the Bible, and in other texts of the ancient world, means loyalty between covenant partners, whether the covenant is political, marital, or religious.

Obedience to God's commandments is the way God's people express their love for Him (6:4–9; 7:9; 10:12–11:1; 30:11–20). But it is also for their good. Under the old covenant, it prolonged life (6:2), increased the nation (6:3), and brought tremendous blessing (7:12–16; 28:1–14).

That may sound confusing to those who have been told that the New Testament, especially Paul's writings, teaches that the old covenant had a "works righteousness"—that it brought condemnation and was not of faith (for example, Rom. 9:32; 2 Cor. 3). But Paul is not criticizing the old covenant; rather, he is criticizing those who put obedience before love, as though they could work their way into a relationship with God. That was never the intention of the old covenant, but unfortunately it had become a characteristic of the Judaism of Paul's day.

Deuteronomy helps us to see that Yahweh intended this covenant for His glory as well as His people's benefit. Because Yahweh loved them, they could love Him (7:7–11). Because Yahweh is good, His covenant brought good to them (6:2, 18). Because Yahweh is righteous, obedience helped them share in His righteousness (6:25).

So as you read Deuteronomy, rejoice in God's goodness to His people. Understand how David could say: "Oh, how I love your law! I meditate on it all day long" (Psalm 119:97). Praise God for the greater blessings of the New Covenant, a covenant that has no curse or condemnation for those who are in Christ.

JOSHUA

Author: Joshua

Date: 1400–1370 B.C. The events of Joshua begin where those of Deuteronomy concluded. They describe the conquest and division of the land of

Canaan, and are set against the backdrop of the corrupt and brutal features of Canaanite religion.

Theme: Disobedience of God's commands can lead to spiritual decline. Much of the later spiritual declension in Israel was due to the Israelites not completely destroying the Canaanites as God had commanded. As a result, the foreign religion was tolerated and frequently absorbed by the Israelites.

Overview: The first twelve chapters of Joshua narrate the conquest of Canaan, about 1406–1400 B.C., whereas chapters 13–24 relate the division of the land among the tribes. Contrary to Numbers, which precedes it, and Judges, which follows it, Joshua emphasizes that Yahweh blesses His people when they obey Him.

But Joshua also illustrates that a little disobedience goes a long way. Though Israel conquers Jericho, the people are defeated at Ai because of Achan's sin (chapters 6–7). They renew the covenant on Mount Ebal, then violate it by making a covenant with the Gibeonites (8:30–9:27). They conquer most of the land, but every tribe has pockets of resistance that it has failed to overcome (for example, 15:63; 16:10; 17:12–13). Allowing the Canaanites to remain in the land results in the apostasy and anarchy of the period of judges, as the gods of Canaan fight with Yahweh, God of Israel, for supremacy in the hearts of His people.

This concept of commitment, of love for Yahweh, is emphasized in the events and oration of chapters 22–24. As you read Joshua, examine your own heart to see what areas still need to be conquered to make you wholehearted in your love for God.

Going Deeper . . .

"It's sad but true that the average person thinks that reading the Bible is dreadfully boring," writes Howard Hendricks in *Living by the Book.* Some of the history prior to the establishment of the monarchy may seem like boring reading, but there are ways you can make it come alive. Read part 2 of the "Ten Strategies for First-Rate Reading" (on page 64) to learn three more strategies to enhance your reading of Scripture, including asking the who, what, where, when, why, and wherefore questions.

April

In those days Israel had no king; everyone did as he saw fit.
—Judges 17:6

BIBLE READING SCHEDULE

DATE	TEXT	DATE	TEXT
April 1	Judges 2–5	**April 18**	1 Sam. 24; Ps. 57; 1 Sam. 25
April 2	Judges 6–8	**April 19**	1 Sam. 26–29; 1 Chron. 12:1-7, 19–22
April 3	Judges 9		
April 4	Judges 10–12	**April 20**	1 Sam. 30–31; 1 Chron. 10; 2 Sam. 1
April 5	Judges 13–16		
April 6	Judges 17–19	**April 21**	2 Sam. 2–4
April 7	Judges 20–21	**April 22**	2 Sam. 5:1–6:11; 1 Chron. 11:1-9; 12:23-40; 13–14
April 8	Ruth		
April 9	1 Sam. 1–3	**April 23**	2 Sam. 22; Ps. 18
April 10	1 Sam. 4–7	**April 24**	1 Chron. 15–16; 2 Sam. 6:12–23; Ps. 96
April 11	1 Sam. 8–10		
April 12	1 Sam. 11–13	**April 25**	Ps. 105; 2 Sam. 7; 1 Chron. 17
April 13	1 Sam. 14–15	**April 26**	2 Sam. 8–10; 1 Chron. 18–19; Ps. 60
April 14	1 Sam. 16–17		
April 15	1 Sam. 18–19; Ps. 59	**April 27**	2 Sam. 11–12; 1 Chron. 20:1-3; Ps. 51
April 16	1 Sam. 20–21; Ps. 56; 34		
April 17	1 Sam. 22–23; 1 Chron. 12:8–18; Pss. 52; 54; 63; 142	**April 28**	2 Sam. 13–14
		April 29	2 Sam. 15–17
		April 30	Ps. 3; 2 Sam. 18–19

Getting to Know . . .

JUDGES

Author: Anonymous. The Talmud suggests Samuel, and it is possible that he may have written portions.

Date: 1050–1000 B.C. The events of this book cover the turbulent period in Israel's history from about 1380 to 1050 B.C., from the conquests of Palestine to the beginnings of the monarchy.

Background: Though the land had been generally conquered and occupied under Joshua, many important Canaanite strongholds had been bypassed, leaving their subjugation to individual Israelite tribes. Judges describes this warfare, as the Hebrews tried to complete their occupation of the land. The judges were military and civil leaders ruling during this time when the nation was a loose confederacy. Some of the judges ruled concurrently, since each one did not necessarily rule over the entire land.

Overview: Deuteronomy set out the blessings and curses of the covenant at Sinai—blessing for obedience to the will of Yahweh, and a curse for disobedience. The book of Joshua illustrates God's blessing; Israel entered the land by faith and conquered it by God's power. Judges, on the other hand, illustrates God's curse.

Joshua begins and ends with a charge to the people of Israel to claim life and blessing by committing themselves to Yahweh as their only God and by committing themselves to the law as Yahweh's design for success and prosperity. In Judges, Israel soon turns regularly to the gods of the nations, and the word *law* never occurs. Rather, "everyone did as he saw fit," or "did that which was right in his own eyes" (17:6; 21:25, KJV).

The cycle of the book of Judges is outlined in 2:10–19: The people forsake Yahweh for other gods; Yahweh judges them, using an oppressive nation; the people repent and cry out for deliverance; Yahweh raises a judge (a military and political savior); the land and the people rest in peace. But the pattern is not just a cycle—it's a downward spiral. Each time the people come full circle they are a notch lower than the time before.

That declining state can also be seen in the judges. The line begins with Othniel, whose sole recorded contribution was a military victory that brought forty years of peace; it ends with Samson, who never responded to God's commands. Though we sometimes glorify Samson in Sunday school stories, the only good he served Israel was to kill the many Philistines who had the bad sense to get in his way. Only twice did he pray, both times in his own interest (15:18–19; 16:28). Samson's epitaph, "he killed many more when he died than while he lived" (16:30), may say he was more useful dead than alive—a sobering reminder of squandered God-given potential.

The last five chapters of Judges, a nauseating account of Levitical idolatry, rape, murder, and intertribal war, bring us to the era of the early monarchy and 1 Samuel (about 1050 B.C.). But nestled between the disappointing ending of Judges and the dismal beginning of Samuel is the remarkable book of Ruth.

RUTH

Author: Uncertain. Some have suggested Samuel as a possible author.
Date: ca. 1000 B.C.
Background: The book provides a glimpse into the lives of ordinary, though godly, people during the turbulent period of the judges. It shows an oasis of faithfulness in an age marked by idolatry and unfaithfulness.
Overview: While Israel was forsaking the true God for false ones, the Baals of Canaan, a Moabitess named Ruth left her home, her country, and her gods because of her love for her mother-in-law, Naomi, and Naomi's God, Yahweh.

Naomi provides the key for understanding the book in 1:20–21. She and her husband, Elimelech, deserted Yahweh and His land to make themselves "full" in Moab, but Yahweh brought her back bereft of family. She was "empty" and "bitter." But He also brought her back with Ruth, who—because of her character, her love for Naomi, and her trust in Yahweh—is made "full" by Boaz. Ruth becomes not only full with food (chapter 2), but also full with child (4:13). And Ruth's fullness overflows to Naomi (4:14–17).

Names are instrumental to the plot of Ruth. As to names of God, note especially in Ruth 1:21–22 that Shaddai, the Almighty, normally a source of refuge and provision, brings bitterness and misfortune, and that Yahweh, the saving covenant God, brings emptiness and affliction. Note also that Boaz and his workers greet each other in the name of Yahweh (2:4)—an amazing declaration of faith in the dark days of the judges.

This beautiful love story leads to the throne of Israel, for Ruth gives birth to Obed, the grandfather of David.

SAMUEL AND CHRONICLES

Authors: 1 and 2 Samuel were written by Samuel himself, along with additional authors. 1 and 2 Chronicles probably were written by Ezra the scribe.
Dates: 1 and 2 Samuel were written approximately 930 B.C., and parts were written some years later. Meanwhile 1 and 2 Chronicles were written between 450 and 425 B.C.
Background: Samuel emerged as the last judge in the 350-year span of the judges. His books cover a period of about 115 years, from the childhood of Samuel to the beginning of the reign of King David. Appearing on the scene

during one of the darkest periods of Israel's history, Samuel called the people to a revival of the true worship of Yahweh. He was also a kingmaker, anointing both Saul (1 Sam. 10:1) and David (1 Sam. 16:13). Thus, 1 Samuel forms the link between the judges and the monarchy.

Looking at 1 and 2 Chronicles, we know that Ezra led a group of exiles back to Palestine in 458 B.C. and was concerned about building a true spiritual foundation for the people. To further that purpose, the author evidently compiled the Chronicles in order to emphasize the importance of racial and religious purity, the proper place of the law, the temple, and the priesthood. Thus he omits detailed activities of the kings and prophets, stressing instead the rich heritage of the people and the blessing of their covenant relationship with God.

Overview: Our Bible reading thus far, with the exception of Job, has taken us in the traditional, canonical order. Now the page-flipping will begin, as we integrate the "parallel passages" of Samuel and 1 Chronicle with Psalms.

The books of Samuel begin with Samuel's birth (about 1105 B.C.) and end with the last year of David's reign (about 970 B.C.). As you read, note the character contrasts: Elkanah's two wives—the nag versus the woman of faith; the godly Samuel versus the wicked sons of Eli; spiritual David versus physical Saul; even David's godliness versus David's fleshly passions.

Also note conflicts on the theological level. In Judges 2:11 we were introduced to the conflict of Yahweh, the God of Israel, and Baal, the god of Canaan. This conflict grows in Samuel, peaks at the Mount Carmel incident recorded in Kings, and is finally cut off by the exile. Though Israel continually forgot the reality of Yahweh's power, even to the point of losing the Ark of the Covenant (1 Sam. 4), Yahweh displayed His power among the Philistines by demolishing their gods and inflicting plagues on the people.

Many scholars believe Samuel and Kings were written by prophets, who drew on the court annals of Judah and Israel to put together a history that explained how Israel worked its way into exile. They show Israel's kings, especially David, "warts and all." That demonstrates that while God both rewarded their faith and judged their rebellions, He never gave them up.

Chronicles, on the other hand, emphasizes the acts of faith without totally overlooking the sins. The books of Chronicles were written by Ezra or the priests, who together were encouraging the people to rebuild Jerusalem and realign themselves with God's plan for His people. They emphasize successes rather than failures, to the degree that the sins of David and the rebellious northern kingdom are hardly mentioned at all. Samuel and Chronicles differ in what they include from the life of David.

Though Samuel does not gloss over David's sins, David's heart for God is clearly seen. That is especially true in the magnificent Psalms of the wilderness, which have been interwoven into the readings. As you read these hymnic treasures, rejoice in the fact that the God who loved, protected, and forgave David does the very same for us through Jesus the Messiah.

Going Deeper . . .

Four more strategies for effective reading of the Scriptures can be found in Part 3 of "Ten Strategies for First-Rate Reading" (page 66).

May

May the words of my mouth and the meditation of my heart
be pleasing in your sight, O Lord, my Rock and my Redeemer.
—Psalm 19:14

BIBLE READING SCHEDULE

DATE	TEXT
May 1	2 Sam. 20–21; 23:8–23; 1 Chron. 20:4–8; 11:10–25
May 2	2 Sam. 23:24–24:25; 1 Chron. 11:26–47; 21:1–30
May 3	1 Chron. 22–24
May 4	Ps. 30; 1 Chron. 25–26
May 5	1 Chron. 27–29
May 6	Pss. 5–7; 10; 11; 13; 17
May 7	Pss. 23; 26; 28; 31; 35
May 8	Pss. 41; 43; 46; 55; 61; 62; 64
May 9	Pss. 69–71; 77
May 10	Pss. 83; 86; 88; 91; 95
May 11	Pss. 108–109; 120–121; 140; 143–144
May 12	Pss. 1; 14–15; 36–37; 39
May 13	Pss. 40; 49–50; 73
May 14	Pss. 76; 82; 84; 90; 92; 112; 115
May 15	Pss. 8–9; 16; 19; 21; 24; 29

DATE	TEXT
May 16	Pss. 33; 65–68
May 17	Pss. 75; 93–94; 97–100
May 18	Pss. 103–104; 113–14; 117
May 19	Ps. 119:1–88
May 20	Ps. 119:89–176
May 21	Pss. 122; 124; 133–136
May 22	Pss. 139–139; 145; 148; 150
May 23	Pss. 4; 12; 20; 25; 32; 38
May 24	Pss. 42; 53; 58; 81; 101; 111; 130–131; 141; 146
May 25	Pss. 2; 22; 27
May 26	Pss. 45; 47–48; 87; 110
May 27	1 Kings 1:1–2:12; 2 Sam. 23:1–7
May 28	1 Kings 2:13–3:28; 2 Chron. 1:1–13
May 29	1 Kings 5–6; 2 Chron. 2–3
May 30	1 Kings 7; 2 Chron. 4
May 31	1 Kings 8; 2 Chron. 5:1–7:10

Getting to Know . . .

Psalms

Authors: Various, including David, Solomon, Asaph, the sons of Korah, and more.

Dates: Various

Background: Unlike much of Western poetry, Hebrew poetry is not based on rhyme or meter, but on rhythm and parallelism. The *rhythm* is not achieved by balanced numbers of accented and unaccented syllables, but by tonal stress or accent on important words. In *parallelism*, the poet states an idea in the first line, then reinforces it by various means in the succeeding line or lines. The most common type is synonymous parallelism, in which the second line essentially repeats the idea of the first (3:1).

Overview: If there is any portion of the Old Testament that all Christians read, it is Psalms. There the character of God is more clearly and dramatically proclaimed than in any other Bible book. *Adonay,* "Lord," occurs 63 times. Other words for God appear 427 times, and the name *Yahweh* appears 742 times.

The word *psalm* means music from, or accompanied by, a stringed instrument, which is the way David and others originally sang them. The Hebrew title, however, is *tehillim,* which means "praises." Psalms is indeed the praise book of the Bible.

So what is praise? When we examine the Hebrew word for praise, *hallelujah,* we begin to understand. The *hallel* part is a plural command, meaning something we must do together, in public. Further, praise is not the same as thanks. The meaning of *halal* is to proclaim or declare, to speak about God rather than to thank Him for something. The object of praise is the *jah* part, which is an abbreviated form of the name Yahweh.

In short, *praise is joyfully proclaiming, in public, the attributes of God and the acts of God.* It is speaking about what God is like and what He does. That's why David can praise God even when he is in desperate trouble. Praise is not saying, "Thanks, God, for this lousy situation." Rather, praise is saying, "God is good and will see me through this lousy situation." The Bible contains no "Praise the Lord, anyway" responses, only "Praise the Lord because . . ."

Each of the 150 psalms praises God. And none sums it up better than Psalm 113. Who deserves praise? The psalm begins and ends with "Hallelu-Yah"—"Praise Yahweh!" When is it proper to praise Yahweh? "Both now and forevermore" (v. 2). Where should Yahweh be praised? "From the rising of the sun to the place where it sets" (v. 3). In other words, Yahweh deserves the praise of His people at all times, from every place, and in all situations.

Psalm 113 is a psalm of descriptive praise. It calls people to praise Yahweh for one of His outstanding attributes, in this case because He stoops from the heavens to exalt His people. Psalm 142, on the other hand, is a psalm of lament, a prayer for salvation from a desperate situation. David teaches us that we can cry out to God boldly from the depths of turmoil and be absolutely honest about our feelings and needs. But he also teaches us that we need to know the character of God so that what we request of Him is indeed in line with who He is and what He does. Then we can ask with confidence and security.

Psalm 30 is a psalm of narrative praise, a hymn that praises God for answering a request for salvation. It recalls the deep need from which David cried for help. It also recalls the faithfulness with which God answered—faithfulness to His own character as well as to His relationship with David. It calls all who hear to praise God continually for His goodness and mercy.

When Yahweh revealed His name in Exodus 3, He declared, "This is my name forever, the name by which I am to be remembered from generation to generation" (v. 15). By praising God, we remember Him. When we remember Him, we avoid Israel's error (seen especially in Judges) of forgetting and forsaking God. No wonder "Hallelu-Yah" is the most common command in the Bible.

As you read, watch for these titles of God: King (20 times), Rock (20), Savior/Salvation (19), Fortress (16), *Yahweh* of Hosts/God of Hosts (14), Refuge (13), Shield (12), One Enthroned (11), Help/Helper (10), Strength (9), Maker (7), Stronghold (6), Deliverer (5), Holy One (4), Judge (3), Loving God (3), Portion (3), Shepherd (3), Dwelling Place (2), Father (2), Glory/Glorious One (2), Mighty One of Jacob (2), and Redeemer (2).

KINGS AND CHRONICLES

Author: 1 and 2 Kings were written by Jeremiah.

Date: 1 and 2 Kings were written circa 550 B.C.

Background: Originally one book, 1 and 2 Kings were written not only to record the history of the kings of Israel, but to show that the success of any king (and of the nation as a whole) depended on the measure of his allegiance to God's law. Failure to follow God resulted in decline and captivity.

Overview: We now begin the portions of Kings and Chronicles that describe the transition from David to Solomon. After the building of the temple and Solomon's magnificent prayer of dedication, Yahweh reiterates the covenant He made with David, promising to bless Solomon richly for obedience but to curse the nation for his disobedience—a familiar concept.

At first Solomon responds magnificently. His wealth and wisdom become so legendary that kings and queens travel thousands of miles to seek his favor. Yahweh's will for His people is somewhat fulfilled as their borders extend to the land promised in Numbers and Joshua. They enjoy prosperity and peace. Israel is the center of the world, a kingdom on earth displaying the kingdom of heaven. It is during that era that Solomon collects and composes the "three thousand proverbs" and "thousand and five songs" he is credited with in 1 Kings 4:32.

Note that Chronicles does not parallel 1 Kings 11, which tells of the beginning of the end of Solomon's glory. For every princess that Solomon adds to his harem—which was one of the ways royalty made treaties and agreements—he also adds a competitive god to Yahweh. Eventually his wives lead him astray. Similar to the period of the judges, when Solomon forsakes devotion to Yahweh, Yahweh raises adversaries against him.

With the passing of Solomon comes the passing of Israel's united kingdom. The books of 1 and 2 Kings interweave the history of Israel in the north and Judah in the south. It finds favor and fault in the kings of both regions. Chronicles all but ignores the north, finding great good in most of the kings of Judah but saying nothing good about Israel.

Because of these perspectives, we will read parallel accounts of all the kings of Judah, but only the books of 1 and 2 Kings will elaborate on Israel and, because of the location of their ministries, on Elijah and Elisha. In that connection, note the climactic confrontation between Yahweh and Baal on Mount Carmel in 1 Kings 18.

Later in Israel's history (835 B.C.) when Joash takes the throne, it is Chronicles that brings out the wickedness of the latter part of Joash's reign. Most likely that is because Joash's great sins were abandoning the temple and murdering Zechariah, a priest, and Chronicles was probably recorded by priests.

The only noteworthy king of the northern kingdom (again noted only in Kings) in the final century of Israel's existence was Jeroboam II. His forty-year reign (793–753 B.C.) brought unparalleled peace and prosperity but also unparalleled greed and idolatry among the upper class. The self-centeredness of that generation spawned the strong prophecies of Hosea, Amos, and Jonah.

In Judah, the good kings Joash, Amaziah, Uzziah (Azariah), Jotham, and even Hezekiah and Josiah could not measure up to the standard set by David. And wicked kings such as Ahaz, Manasseh, and Amon pushed Judah over the edge, which led them into Babylonian exile in 586 B.C., following Israel's exile to Assyria in 722 B.C.

Going Deeper . . .

Reading the Bible for meaning requires interacting with the text. To learn some basic methods for reading and reflecting on Scripture, read the article "A Proven Method for Studying the Bible" on page 69.

June

The fear of the Lord is the beginning of knowledge,
but fools despise wisdom and discipline.
—Proverbs 1:7

BIBLE READING SCHEDULE

DATE	TEXT	DATE	TEXT
June 1	1 Kings 9:1–10:13; 2 Chron. 7:11–9:12	June 18	1 Kings 12; 2 Chron. 10:1–11:17
June 2	1 Kings 4; 10:14–29; 2 Chron. 1:14–17; 9:13–28; Ps. 72	June 19	1 Kings 13–14; 2 Chron. 11:18–12:16
June 3	Proverbs 1–3	June 20	1 Kings 15:1–24; 2 Chron. 13–16
June 4	Proverbs 4–6		
June 5	Proverbs 7–9	June 21	1 Kings 15:25–16:34; 2 Chron. 17; 1 Kings 17
June 6	Proverbs 10–12		
June 7	Proverbs 13–15	June 22	1 Kings 18–19
June 8	Proverbs 16–18	June 23	1 Kings 20–21
June 9	Proverbs 19–21	June 24	1 Kings 22:1–40; 2 Chron. 18
June 10	Proverbs 22–24	June 25	1 Kings 22:41–53; 2 Kings 1; 2 Chron. 19:1–21:3
June 11	Proverbs 25–27		
June 12	Proverbs 28–29	June 26	2 Kings 2–4
June 13	Proverbs 30–31; Ps. 127	June 27	2 Kings 5–7
June 14	Song of Songs	June 28	2 Kings 8–9; 2 Chron. 21:4–22:9
June 15	1 Kings 11:1–40; Eccles. 1–2		
June 16	Eccles. 3–7	June 29	2 Kings 10–11; 2 Chron. 22:10–23:21
June 17	Eccles. 8–12; 1 Kings 11:41–43; 2 Chron. 9:29–31	June 30	Joel

Getting to Know . . .

PROVERBS

Author: Solomon and others

Date: 950 –700 B.C.

Background: The type of literature found in Proverbs goes back in written form to about 2700 B.C. in Egypt. The Hebrew term for proverb means "a comparison," and it came to be used for any sage or moralistic pronouncement. Many proverbs are condensed parables. The sayings in this book form a library of instruction on how to live a godly life here on earth, and how to be assured of reward in the life to come. Thus, these proverbs are not so much popular sayings as they are a distillation of wisdom from those who knew the law of God.

Overview: In Job we were introduced to the concept of "wisdom literature." Common to all civilizations, wisdom literature represents the attempt of human beings to observe God's creation, to discern its order and its workings, and to synthesize those observations into concise, memorable statements of truth. Because God is a God of order, there is also order to the universe, which can be perceived and described.

In wisdom literature, more than any other, we come to realize that all truth is God's truth. Unique to Proverbs, however, is the fear of Yahweh, which is the beginning of knowledge and motto of the book (1:7).

Fear of Yahweh does not mean being scared of God; it means regarding Him with reverence. If you fear Yahweh, you will want to be like Him. Thus, one aspect of fear is to turn from evil (8:13). Another is to increase in knowledge of God and intimacy with him (9:10). One benefit of the fear of Yahweh is a successful life (10:27; 19:23). While other wisdom literature may deal truthfully with God's creation, only the wisdom of Israel deals truthfully with God Himself.

Proverbs provides experience and observation in capsule form. It speaks of patterns rather than absolutes. Though the proverbs seem so simple, they all have hidden contexts and exceptions.

Think about the well-known American proverb "A stitch in time saves nine." Is it correct? Yes—it captures well the second law of thermodynamics, that things tend to fall apart rather than come together. But does it teach that if you do not fix something today, it will be nine times worse tomorrow? Of course not! It simply means things fall into a worse state rather than a better one. "Nine" rhymes somewhat with "time" to make the proverb memorable.

SONG OF SONGS

Author: Solomon

Date: Circa 965 B.C.

Purpose: The purpose behind the Song of Songs has become a controversial topic in theological circles. Some scholars regard this book purely as an allegory, meaning that fictional characters are employed to teach the truth of God's love for His people. Such a nonhistorical view, however, is contrary to all principles of normal interpretation and must be rejected. Others rightly understand the book to be a historical record of the romance of Solomon with a Shulammite woman. The "snapshots" in the book portray the joys of love in courtship and marriage; they also counteract the extremes of both asceticism and lust. The rightful place of physical love, within marriage only, is clearly established and honored.

Overview: Much as the Holy of Holies in Solomon's temple was the holiest of all places on earth, so the Song of Songs is the greatest of Solomon's songs. It unashamedly praises monogamous love, the love of one woman and one man.

There are dozens of variations in understanding the poem's plot and movement. But the point is still clear—the best love is faithful love, the kind that cannot be seduced by power and wealth. Although the song uses no names of God, it is fitting that the rabbis allegorized the song as Yahweh's love for Israel, and the church fathers looked to it as Christ's love for His church; for whether on a secular or a spiritual plane, love is fidelity.

ECCLESIASTES

Author: Solomon

Date: Circa 935 B.C.

Purpose: The message of Ecclesiastes may be stated in the form of three propositions:

1. When you look at life with its seemingly aimless cycles (1:4ff) and inexplicable paradoxes (4:1; 7:15; 8:8), you might conclude that all is futile, since it is impossible to discern any purpose in the ordering of events.
2. Nevertheless, life is to be enjoyed to the fullest, realizing that it is the gift of God (3:12–13, 22; 5:18–19; 8:15; 9:7–9).
3. The wise man will live his life in obedience to God, recognizing that God will eventually judge all men (3:16–17; 12:14).

Overview: Ecclesiastes is traditionally ascribed to Solomon during his latter years. It is usually understood as a pessimistic and even secular reflection on the futility of life. But in truth, Ecclesiastes offers profound and unparalleled information on the nature of true happiness.

The "Teacher" or "Preacher" who narrates the poem describes life "under the sun" as meaningless—as "vanity" or "vapor." He tries every way "under the sun" of finding meaning and happiness but finds nothing but pain. He refers to God only by the basic term Elohim, never by the covenant name Yahweh, which cannot be perceived "under the sun"—without God's self-revelation.

The Teacher was unusually observant. He could not ignore the exceptions to wisdom: the righteous dying young, servants ruling masters, the wicked escaping punishment. He tried to find a way of life "under the sun," that is, one that did not honor the God who is "over the sun"—the God who has created the world and revealed His will. But every alternate avenue was a dead end.

Yet, in all his searching, the Teacher concluded that there is indeed adequate good and that God has given people plenty to enjoy: the benefits of the norms outnumber the seeming injustices of the exceptions. Thus he encourages wisdom over folly, discipline over excess, and obedience to God over self-centeredness.

"Under the sun," we cannot perceive all of God's purpose. But we can trust that He is good and that His will, in the long run, will triumph. If we, too, concentrate on the norms rather than the exceptions, we will enjoy the life God intends.

JOEL

Author: Joel

Date: 835 B.C.

Themes: The major theme of Joel's prophecy is the "day of the Lord"—God's special intervention in the affairs of human history. Three facets of the day of the Lord are discernable:

1. *The historical.* That is, God's intervention in the affairs of Israel (Zephaniah 1:14–18; Joel 1:15) and in the affairs of heathen nations (Isaiah 13:6; Jeremiah 46:10; Ezekiel 30:3).
2. *The illustrative.* This is where an historical incident represents a partial fulfillment, or an illustration, of the eschatological day of the Lord (Joel 2:1–11; Isaiah 13:6–13).
3. *The eschatological.* This eschatological "day" includes the time of the Great Tribulation (Isaiah 4:2; 12; 19:23–25; Jeremiah 30:7–9).

Overview: Through Joel, *Yahweh* communicates the importance of worshiping Him in spirit and in truth, in the way God prescribes. Israel was not sacrificing or attending to the temple properly, so God brought a locust plague to destroy staples in the land. When the people saw what they were missing, they realized how they had been neglecting Yahweh.

Primarily preachers, the prophets were sent by God to turn their contemporaries back to right living by proclaiming the law. Likewise, Joel's primary message was to his contemporaries. Today as we read about "the day of the Lord" in Joel, we get excited about Pentecost and Armageddon. But as we begin to read the prophets, don't miss the significance of Joel's preaching—and that of the other prophets—to his own generation. We must not be so future oriented that we miss opportunity for current good.

Going Deeper . . .

June means summer is here. Enjoy the increased activities this season brings—perhaps even a vacation or two! During this time, continue to read the Scriptures daily. Be disciplined in reading the Bible day by day. To help you toward the goal, there will be no "Going Deeper" readings during June and July. But keep on reading the Scriptures!

July

He has showed you, O man, what is good. And what does the Lord require of
you? To act justly and to love mercy and to walk humbly with your God.
—Micah 6:8

BIBLE READING SCHEDULE

DATE	TEXT	DATE	TEXT
July 1	2 Kings 12–13; 2 Chron. 24	**July 17**	2 Kings 18:1–8; 2 Chron. 29–31
July 2	2 Kings 14; 2 Chron. 25; Jonah	**July 18**	2 Kings 17; 18:9–37; 2 Chron. 32:1–19; Isa. 36
July 3	Hosea 1–7	**July 19**	2 Kings 19; 2 Chron. 32:20–23; Isa. 37
July 4	Hosea 8–14	**July 20**	2 Kings 20; 2 Chron. 32:24–33; Isa. 38–39
July 5	2 Kings 15:1–7; 2 Chron. 26; Amos 1–4	**July 21**	2 Kings 21:1–18; 2 Chron. 33:1–20; Isa. 40
July 6	Amos 5–9; 2 Kings 15:8–18	**July 22**	Isa. 41–43
July 7	Isa. 1–4	**July 23**	Isa. 44–47
July 8	2 Kings 15:19–38; 2 Chron. 27; Isa. 5–6	**July 24**	Isa. 48–51
July 9	Micah	**July 25**	Isa. 52–57
July 10	2 Kings 16; 2 Chron. 28; Isa. 7–8	**July 26**	Isa. 58–62
July 11	Isa. 9–12	**July 27**	Isa. 63–66
July 12	Isa. 13–16	**July 28**	2 Kings 21:19–26; 2 Chron. 33:21–34:7; Zephaniah
July 13	Isa. 17–22	**July 29**	Jer. 1–3
July 14	Isa. 23–27	**July 30**	Jer. 4–6
July 15	Isa. 28–30	**July 31**	Jer. 7–9
July 16	Isa. 31–35		

Getting to Know . . .

JONAH

Author: Jonah

Date: 760 B.C.

Background: No Assyrian inscription mentions a religious awakening such as that described in this book. However, during the reign of Adad-nirari III (810–783 B.C.) there was a swing toward monotheism, which may have been the result of Jonah's preaching. Or the awakening may have occurred in the days of Ashurdan III (771–754 B.C.).

Overview: During the two-and-one-half centuries from King Joash to Israel's exile, the prophets stood alone as God's watchmen and spokesmen. Today we tend to read the prophets for their predictions—to us, "prophecy" means "prediction." Biblical prophecy, however, is not so much foretelling as forthtelling. A prophet was a preacher designated by God to rebuke Israel and Judah for violating their covenant with Yahweh; he was to warn them of the consequences of continued disobedience and to remind them of the promised blessings of loyalty to Yahweh and the covenant.

Second Kings 14:25 indicates that Jonah predicted the enormity and success of Jeroboam II's kingdom. Perhaps Jonah, too, had bought into the prosperity and complacency that the upper class enjoyed and thus was unwilling to take Yahweh's message of salvation to Nineveh. But God literally moved heaven and earth to get His prophet and His message to Nineveh, and in the process He saved everyone who came into contact with Jonah.

HOSEA

Author: Hosea

Date: Circa 710 B.C.

Background: All we know about the prophet Hosea comes from the autobiographical sections of his book. Like his contemporary Amos, he prophesied to the northern kingdom—also known as Israel, and sometimes as Ephraim—while Isaiah and Micah were ministering to the southern kingdom (Judah). Material prosperity and spiritual bankruptcy characterized the time under Jeroboam II, when Hosea began his ministry (2 Kings 14:23–17:41). Judgment seemed remote, but by 732 B.C. Damascus had fallen to the Assyrians, and by 722, Samaria, the capital of Israel, fell. As a result, the people were deported.

Overview: While Jonah (eventually) preached to those in Nineveh, Hosea and Amos prophesied to the northern kingdom (760–720 B.C.). Hosea's painful marriage to the harlot Gomer is a picture of Yahweh's long-suffering loyalty to Israel, despite Israel's extreme disloyalty.

Chapters 4–14 are a lawsuit against Israel for breaking the covenant.

Though "there is no faithfulness, no love, no acknowledgment of God in the land" (4:1), Yahweh remains faithful in loving and acknowledging His people. Though they must be disciplined through exile, Yahweh will restore them.

AMOS

Author: Amos
Date: 755 B.C.
Background: Amos was a southerner from Tekoa, a village ten miles south of Jerusalem, who traveled north to Bethel in order to preach on what was virtually foreign soil to him. Though a layman, not a professional prophet, he had a direct call of God to his work (7:15). By occupation he was a sheep breeder, perhaps a master shepherd with others in his employ. Amos's preaching in Bethel, a center of idol worship and the residence of the reigning king, Jeroboam II, aroused such opposition that he returned to Judah, where he committed his message to writing. That writing shows that he was a man of affairs, not an untutored rustic.

Overview: Amos is almost exclusively a book of severe judgment against Israel for turning from Yahweh to idols, and for oppressing the poor and needy. His favorite designation of God is *Adonay Yahweh*, which can be translated as "Lord God" or "Sovereign LORD." This emphasized to the Israelites that the God of the covenant was not only their intimate Savior, but also their sovereign Master.

The only word of hope comes at the end of the book (9:11–15), where God promises not only to restore Israel and its king in time, but also to call together all nations that bear His name. It is that passage of Scripture that showed the early church that Gentiles could become Christians without becoming Jewish proselytes (Acts 15:16–17).

ISAIAH

Author: Isaiah
Date: 740–680 B.C.
Theme: Isaiah has often been called "the evangelical prophet" because he says so much about the redemptive work of the future Messiah. More about the person and work of Christ is found here than in any other book of the Old Testament. Consequently, there are many important and favorite passes in this book, some of which are: 1:18; 2:4; 6:3, 8; 7:14; 9:6–7; 11:9; 26:3; 35:1; 40:3; 48:16; chapter 53; 57:15; 59:1; and 61:1–3.
Overview: Isaiah and Micah were contemporaries (740–685 B.C.), both ministering to Judah. In fact, Isaiah 2:1–4 and Micah 4:1–3 are identical. Both prophesied judgment and hope to Judah before and following the fall of Israel to the Assyrians.

Isaiah is best known for his messianic prophecies, as in chapter 53. But most of his message was geared to turning Judah from its collision course with the judgment of exile. Chapters 40–66 anticipate the postexilic restoration of the Jewish nation and describes the superiority of *Yahweh* to the gods of other nations. These chapters also point to the message and ministry of *Yahweh's* Spirit-anointed Servant, the Messiah, who would suffer and die for the sins of the nation, and the necessity to seek Yahweh on His terms in order to enter His kingdom.

MICAH

Author: Micah
Date: 700 B.C.
Background: Micah ministered during the reigns of Jotham (750–732 B.C.), Ahaz (736–716), and Hezekiah (716–687). For the peasants and villagers of the southern kingdom, these were days of harassment from enemy armies, of hardship because of exploitation by the wealthy (2:1–13), and of oppression by the rulers (3:1–4) and false prophets (3:5–8). Throughout all of this, Micah—like Amos—cried for social justice.
Overview: Micah's judgments primarily centered on the leaders of Judah—the prophets, rulers, elders, and priests. He contrasted their abuse of *Yahweh's* flock with the Good Shepherd, who would rule with strength and in peace (5:1–5).

Micah also succinctly summarized the godly life that all followers of God should strive for: "He has showed you, O man, what is good. And what does the Lord [*Yahweh*] require of you? To act justly and to love mercy and to walk humbly with your God" (6:8).

ZEPHANIAH

Author: Zephaniah
Date: Circa 625 B.C.
Background: Zephaniah was a man of noble birth (1:1), and his ministry helped prepare Judah for the revival that took place under good King Josiah in 621 B.C. (2 Chronicles 34:3). For more than half a century, times had been evil under kings Manasseh and Amon, and Zephaniah called his people to repentance. Reform did come—for a time. But after Josiah, the leaders and many of the people reverted back to their old ways.
Overview: Almost a century after Isaiah and Micah, Zephaniah, like Joel, prophesied about the coming destruction of the day of Yahweh—"the day of the Lord"—when He would judge the wicked among the nations and the rebellious within Israel and Judah. Only those who seek *Yahweh*, who seek righteousness and humility, will be sheltered on that day (2:3). Zephaniah's message certainly affected Josiah (640–609 B.C.), whose reforms were second only to King Hezekiah's.

August

See, he is puffed up; his desires are not upright—
but the righteous will live by his faith.
—Habakkuk 2:4

BIBLE READING SCHEDULE

DATE	TEXT
Aug. 1	Jer. 10–13
Aug. 2	Jer. 14–16
Aug. 3	Jer. 17–20
Aug. 4	2 Kings 22:1–23:28; 2 Chron. 34:8–35:19
Aug. 5	Nahum; 2 Kings 23:29–37; 2 Chron. 35:20–36:5; Jer. 22:10–17
Aug. 6	Jer. 26; Habakkuk
Aug. 7	Jer. 46–47; 2 Kings 24:1–4, 7; 2 Chron. 36:6–7; Jer. 25, 35
Aug. 8	Jer. 36, 45, 48
Aug. 9	Jer. 49:1–33; Dan. 1–2
Aug. 10	Jer. 22:18–30; 2 Kings 24:5–20; 2 Chron. 36:8–12; Jer. 37:1–2; 52:1–3; 24; 29
Aug. 11	Jer. 27–28, 23
Aug. 12	Jer. 50–51
Aug. 13	Jer. 49:34–39; 34; Ezek. 1–3
Aug. 14	Ezek. 4–7
Aug. 15	Ezek. 8–11
Aug. 16	Ezek. 12–14

DATE	TEXT
Aug. 17	Ezek. 15–17
Aug. 18	Ezek. 18–20
Aug. 19	Ezek. 21–23
Aug. 20	2 Kings 25:1; 2 Chron. 36:13–16; Jer. 39:1; 52:4; Ezek. 24; Jer. 21:1–22:9; 32
Aug. 21	Jer. 30–31, 33
Aug. 22	Ezek. 25; 29:1–16; 30; 31
Aug. 23	Ezek. 26–28
Aug. 24	Jer. 37:3–39:10; 52:4–30; 2 Kings 25:2–21; 2 Chron. 36:17–21
Aug. 25	2 Kings 25:22; Jer. 39:11–40:6; Lam. 1–3
Aug. 26	Lam. 4–5; Obadiah
Aug. 27	Jer. 40:7–44:30; 2 Kings 25:23–26
Aug. 28	Ezek. 33:21–36:38
Aug. 29	Ezek. 37–39
Aug. 30	Ezek. 32:1–33:20; Dan. 3
Aug. 31	Ezek. 40–42

Getting to Know . . .

JEREMIAH

Author: Jeremiah

Date: 627–585 B.C.

Background: Jeremiah began his ministry under good King Josiah, but subsequent kings and the people would oppose him. Sensitive and sympathetic by nature, Jeremiah nevertheless was commanded by God to deliver a stern message of judgment.

Overview: Jeremiah's ministry spanned the generation from King Josiah to the Babylonian exile (627–580 B.C.). In contrast to the other prophets, he encouraged Judah's rulers and people to submit to Yahweh's discipline and surrender to the invading Babylonians. His life displays an incredible struggle and resilience—a determination to serve God in spite of a difficult message, a resistant people, and a lifestyle of pain and persecution.

Our last readings from Kings and Jeremiah are identical, and the final four verses hold extreme significance. Both books are prophetic and judgmental in tone, yet both emphasize that the kingdom of Judah has lasted as long as it has because of *Yahweh's* relationship with David (2 Samuel 7; compare 1 Kings 8:25). Though both books move toward the exile of God's chosen people, both end with Jehoiachin—the last king of Judah—released from prison while in exile (2 Kings 25:27–30; Jeremiah 52:31–34).

What does this mean? On the basis of the old covenant, God is righteously judging His people. On the basis of the Davidic covenant, however, God has not forgotten His king. Because God remains faithful to His word, His people can trust that He will bring them back from exile (Jeremiah 25:8–14).

NAHUM

Author: Nahum

Date: 663–612 B.C.

Background: Nothing is known of Nahum (whose name means "consolation") except that he came from Elkosh, which was possibly Capernaum. His message against Nineveh was given to Judah, since the northern kingdom, Israel, had already been taken captive by the Assyrians.

Overview: Nahum and Habakkuk both prophesied in the last days of the southern kingdom, also known as Judah. Nahum reveled in the well-deserved destruction of Nineveh and the Assyrian Empire (612 B.C.) because of their cruelty to Israel and to all the nations.

On the basis of Exodus 34:6–7a, God had forgiven the Ninevites in the days of Jonah (Jonah 4:2). But now, on the basis of Exodus 34:7b, *Yahweh* would not leave the guilty unpunished (Nahum 1:3).

HABAKKUK

Author: Habakkuk
Date: 606–604 B.C.
Background: Prophesying just before Nebuchadnezzar first invaded Judah in 605 B.C. (and took Daniel and others as captives to Babylon), Habakkuk was commissioned to announced the Lord's intention to punish Judah by the coming deportation into Babylon. Jerusalem's reigning king at that time, Jehoiakim, is described by the prophet Jeremiah this way: "Your eyes and your heart are intent only upon your own dishonest gain, and on shedding innocent blood, and on practicing oppression and extortion" (Jer. 22:17 NASB).
Overview: Habakkuk is best known for saying, "the just shall live by faith" (2:4 KJV). Those words are also quoted in Romans 1:17, Galatians 3:11, and Hebrews 10:37–38. Habakkuk is also known for having a lot of questions. The prophet could not understand how holy and righteous Yahweh could judge Judah with a more wicked nation like Babylon. Yahweh replied that He would justly judge both His people and their oppressors for their wickedness.

Through the course of this exchange, Habakkuk learned a lesson that is still immensely important for us today: in difficult times, even when we fail to see the evidence of God's concern or control, the righteous person lives by faithfulness to God and by trusting in God's faithfulness.

DANIEL

Author: Daniel
Date: 537 B.C.
Background: Though Daniel and others were taken as captives to Babylon (605 B.C.), Daniel's godly insight earned him a place of prominence and responsibility in Nebuchadnezzar's kingdom at Belshazzar's feast (5:13) and later. His ministry, which continued until the third year of Cyrus, was to testify, in his personal life and his prophecies, to the power of God.
Overview: Daniel and his friends, who were exiled in Babylon, were blessed by God for their continued faithfulness to Him and His covenant. God blessed them by increasing their positions and preserving their lives (reminiscent of Joseph in Egypt). Daniel's ministry continued through the end of the Babylonian Empire and into the reign of Persia. Like Mordecai and Esther, he never returned to the promised homeland.

Though the interpretation of the chronology of Daniel's visions draws much speculation and variance of opinion, we can rest confident in the point God is making—His kingdom reigns supremely over all the kingdoms of mankind. We can also take to heart the application: God rewards faithfulness to Him with life and righteousness. Some are preserved alive through persecution, as were Daniel and his friends; others who die in persecution are resurrected to everlasting life.

EZEKIEL

Author: Ezekiel
Date: 592–570 B.C.
Background: Born of a priestly family (1:3), Ezekiel—whose name means "God strengthens"—spent his early years in Jerusalem, until he was taken with other hostages by Nebuchadnezzar to Babylon in 597 B.C. There he settled in his own house in a village near Nippur, along the river Kebar in Babylonia. Ezekiel prophesied for at least twenty-two years (1:2 and 29:17–21). His wife died in 587 (24:16–18).
Overview: Ezekiel begins with not only a breathtaking revelation of God's glory, but also a heartrending vision of that glory departing from the temple in the midst of God's people. In his description of the restored temple, these events are reversed: Ezekiel sees the glory return, never to depart (chapter 43). The last line of the book gives a new name to Jerusalem: "The Lord [*Yahweh*] is there!"

Ezekiel bears many connections to the book of Revelation, including the measuring and description of the city and temple (Ezekiel 40–48; Revelation 21), the resident glory of God (Ezekiel 43:1–5; Revelation 21:22–27), the river from the temple and the trees of healing (Ezekiel 47:1–12; Revelation 22:1–2), and the concepts behind these quotes: "[*Yahweh*] is there" (Ezekiel 48:35) and "The dwelling of God is with men, and he will live with them" (Revelation 21:3).

In his preaching, Ezekiel proclaimed Yahweh's holiness and glory. He also emphasized the need to repent and to trust solely in Yahweh to restore the covenant, the temple, and the glory after the exile. Ezekiel uses *Adonay* 219 times in his book—more than all the historical and prophetic books combined—to demonstrate that Yahweh is still in control, even though His people are in exile and His name is suffering shame. As surely as He has judged His people, He will restore them and judge their enemies in due time.

LAMENTATIONS

Author: Jeremiah
Date: 586–585 B.C.
Background: From 588 to 586 B.C., the Babylonian army besieged Jerusalem (2 Kings 25:1–10). Judah's ally, Egypt, had been defeated, and Jeremiah's repeated warnings to the Jews had been rejected. As Babylon's stranglehold on Jerusalem tightened, people were starving, yet they continued to turn to idols for help. Finally, the walls were breached; the city plundered; the temple,

palace, and other buildings burned; and prisoners deported to Babylon. Having witnessed these horrible events, Jeremiah composed these laments.

Overview: Two books follow the fall of Jerusalem in 586 B.C.—Lamentations and Obadiah. As the title indicates, Lamentations is a lament over the fall of Jerusalem. The first four of its five chapters are acrostics: each verse begins with the successive letter of the Hebrew alphabet. That may indicate the book was intended to be memorized so as never to forget the reasons for and the pain of God's judgment.

OBADIAH

Author: Obadiah

Date: 841 or 586 B.C. The question of date relates to which battle against Jerusalem the Edomites were associated with. There were four significant invasions of Jerusalem in Old Testament times. Obadiah prophesied against Edom either in connection with the second invasion (848–841) or the fourth (605–586).

Background: Descendants of Esau, Jacob's twin, the Edomites were in constant conflict with Israel, the descendants of Jacob. They rejected Moses' request to pass through their land (Numbers 20:14–20), they opposed King Saul (1 Samuel 14:47), they fought against David (1 Kings 11:14–17), they opposed Solomon (1 Kings 11:14–25)) and Jehoshaphat (2 Chronicles 20:22), and rebelled against Jehoram (2 Chronicles 21:8).

Overview: Whereas Jeremiah responds to the fall of Jerusalem with mourning, Obadiah anticipates God's judgment on Edom for the violence of Esau's descendants against their brother Jacob in assisting the invading Babylonians to destroy and enslave Judah. Edom's destruction is seen as an example of the day of Yahweh—the day of the Lord—which will bring judgment on all the enemies of the people of Yahweh.

Going Deeper . . .

There are six kinds of writing, or genres, in the Bible, and they all influence our understanding of what we read. Learn about the first five by reading "What Type of Literature Is This? Part 1" on page 70.

September

Now this is what the Lord Almighty says: "Give careful thought to your ways. You have planted much, but have harvested little. You eat, but never have enough. You drink, but never have your fill. You put on clothes, but are not warm. You earn wages, only to put them in a purse with holes in it."
—Haggai 1:5–6

BIBLE READING SCHEDULE

DATE	TEXT
Sept. 1	Ezek. 43–45
Sept. 2	Ezek. 46–48
Sept. 3	Ezek. 29:17–21; Dan. 4; Jer. 52:31–34; 2 Kings 25:27–30; Ps. 44
Sept. 4	Pss. 74; 79–80; 89
Sept. 5	Pss. 85; 102; 106; 123; 137
Sept. 6	Dan. 7–8; 5
Sept. 7	Dan. 9; 6
Sept. 8	2 Chron. 36:22–23; Ezra 1:1–4:5
Sept. 9	Dan. 10–12
Sept. 10	Ezra 4:6–6:13; Haggai
Sept. 11	Zach. 1–6
Sept. 12	Zach. 7–8; Ezra 6:14–22; Ps. 78
Sept. 13	Pss. 107; 116; 118
Sept. 14	Pss. 125–126; 128–129; 132; 147; 149

DATE	TEXT
Sept. 15	Zach. 9–14
Sept. 16	Esther 1–4
Sept. 17	Esther 5–10
Sept. 18	Ezra 7–8
Sept. 19	Ezra 9–10
Sept. 20	Neh. 1–5
Sept. 21	Neh. 6–7
Sept. 22	Neh. 8–10
Sept. 23	Neh. 11–13
Sept. 24	Malachi
Sept. 25	1 Chron. 1–2
Sept. 26	1 Chron. 3–5
Sept. 27	1 Chron. 6
Sept. 28	1 Chron. 7:1–8:27
Sept. 29	1 Chron. 8:28–9:44
Sept. 30	John 1:1–18; Mark 1:1; Luke 1:1–4; 2:23–38; Matt. 1:1–17

Getting to Know . . .

HAGGAI

Author: Haggai

Date: 520 B.C.

Background: Haggai (whose name means "my feast") was the first prophetic voice to be heard after the Babylonian exile. He was a contemporary of Zechariah (and of Confucius), and his ministry was to call the people to finish the temple, whose completion had been delayed for fifteen years. Haggai likely returned to Jerusalem from Babylon with Zerubbabel.

Overview: In 520 B.C., Haggai proclaimed four messages to the people who had returned to Jerusalem from Babylon. The first rebuked them for paneling their own houses while Yahweh's temple remained a ruin. Yahweh Almighty would withhold blessing until they honored His presence, he told them. Within the month, they began the work.

In the second message, a month later, Yahweh promised to restore His glory to the temple, to restore the line of David (in Zerubbabel the governor), and to restore the priesthood (in Joshua/Jeshua the high priest).

The third message paralleled the first, urging Israel to remember the contrast between the lack of blessing from the people's failure to work on the temple and fullness of blessing from their obedience. The fourth paralleled the second. It proclaimed that God had maintained faithfulness to His covenant with David by preserving His descendants, through Zerubbabel, to rule His people.

ZECHARIAH

Author: Zechariah

Date: 520–518 B.C.

Background: Zechariah's father, Berechiah, probably died when his son was young, making Zechariah the immediate successor of his grandfather, Iddo (Nehemiah 12:4). Iddo was a priest who returned from Babylon with Zerubbabel and Joshua. He was, according to tradition, a member of the Great Synagogue (the governing body of the Jews before the Sanhedrin).

Overview: Zechariah's prophecies began between Haggai's second and third messages. They paralleled the content with eight symbolic visions of restoration and judgment (chapters 1–6). As in Haggai, Zechariah emphasized God's re-establishment of His people, His king, and His priests. But Zechariah also exposed the human and spiritual enemies to God and His people and announced their judgment.

Four years later, Zechariah proclaimed Yahweh's rebuke: The people had fasted because they felt sorry for themselves. Yahweh demanded joyful worship and social justice in His restored community.

The two undated oracles that complete the book are among the most quoted messianic passages of the Old Testament.

ESTHER

Author: Uncertain

Date: Circa 465 B.C.

Background: The events of this book cover a ten-year portion (483–473) of the reign of Xerxes (486–465). Ahasuerus is the Hebrew form of his name. The events take place between those recorded in the sixth and seventh chapters of Ezra.

Overview: As in Ruth, the whole book portrays God as sovereignly interacting in the history of His people. Unlike Ruth, a Moabite in the land of Israel, Esther is an Israelite outside the homeland. Also unlike Ruth, which used the names of God (and of other characters) to explain the events of the book, no name or title of God appears in Esther. God's actions, however, are strongly implied by the many "coincidences" and unusual timing of events.

More than any other book of the Bible, Esther describes God's dealings with His people just as we experience them today. We do not see God or hear His voice, but we see His hand in all things, great and small.

EZRA AND NEHEMIAH

Authors: Ezra and Nehemiah

Date: Ezra was written between 450 and 444 B.C. Nehemiah was written between 445 and 425 B.C.

Background: These books record the fulfillment of God's promise to restore Israel to her land after the seventy years of captivity in Babylon (Jeremiah 25:11). This was accomplished through the help of three Persian kings (Cyrus, Darius, and Artaxerxes) as well as Jewish leaders such as Zerubbabel, Joshua, Haggai, Zechariah, and Ezra. Cyrus overthrew Babylon in October of 539, and in accord with his policy of encouraging subject people to return to their homelands, he issued a decree in 538 allowing the Jews to do the same. About 50,000 Israelites did return under the leadership of Zerubbabel, and the foundation of the temple was laid, although it was not completed until 515 during the reign of Darius.

Overview: The second half of Ezra and the Book of Nehemiah cover how the Jewish leaders direct the rebuilding of the temple, Both books deal with intermarriages with surrounding peoples; Ezra and Nehemiah confront the Israelites about their breach of covenant with Yahweh. Nehemiah further condemns complacent and wicked practices of the priesthood and breaches of the Sabbath.

Most of Nehemiah, however, is concerned with the rebuilding of Jerusalem's wall, done against incredible odds. Nehemiah's commitment to God, his fearless devotion to the protection and purity of God's people, and his personal and prayerful writing style make this book exhilarating and humbling to read.

MALACHI

Author: Malachi
Date: 450–400 B.C.
Background: Malachi ministered approximately one hundred years after the return of the Jews to Palestine. The city of Jerusalem and the second temple had been rebuilt, but initial enthusiasm had worn off. Following a period of revival under Nehemiah, the people and priests had backslidden and become mechanical in their observance of the law. Though lax in their worship (1:7) and delinquent in their tithing (3:8), they could not understand why God was dissatisfied with them.

Overview: Some scholars believe that Malachi's prophecies are not conclusively dated, and that they may even be anonymous, as *Malachi* means "my messenger" (2:7; 3:1). Malachi also sounds somewhat like a preexilic prophet, for he proclaims judgment more than hope.

In dialogue fashion, *Yahweh* contends that His people have not returned His love or honored His holy presence in their marriages, worship, and tithes. Thus, as in the days of Joel, the day of *Yahweh* and the covenant messenger will bring the nation judgment and purification, not joy and salvation. In this book, Old Testament history closes with the expectation of Elijah and his message of restoration.

Going Deeper

Haggai, Zechariah, and Malachi all were prophets. God charged his prophets not only with speaking about the future but also with declaring the present state of affairs, often as a warning to disobedient listeners. As Howard Hendricks explains, "The role of the prophet in Scripture was not so much to tell the future, but to proclaim the words of the Lord; not to foretell, but to 'forth-tell.'" Read his insightful article "Prophecy and Apocalyptic Literature," part 2 of "What Kind of Literature Is This?" on page 75.

October

The Word became flesh and made his dwelling among us.
We have seen his glory, the glory of the One and Only,
who came from the Father, full of grace and truth.
—John 1:14

BIBLE READING SCHEDULE

DATE	TEXT
Oct. 1	Luke 1:5–80
Oct. 2	Matt. 1:18–2:23; Luke 2
Oct. 3	Matt. 3:1–4:11; Mark 1:2–13; Luke 3–4:13; John 1:19–34
Oct. 4	John 1:35–3:36
Oct. 5	John 4; Matt. 4:12–17; Mark 1:14–15; Luke 4:14–30
Oct. 6	Mark 1:16–45; Matt. 4:18–25; 8:2–4, 14–17; Luke 4:31–5:16
Oct. 7	Matt. 9:1–17; Mark 2:1–22; Luke 5:17–39
Oct. 8	John 5; Matt. 12:1–21; Mark 2:23–3:12; Luke 6:1–11
Oct. 9	Matt. 5; Mark 3:13–19; Luke 6:12–36
Oct. 10	Matt. 6–7; Luke 6:37–49
Oct. 11	Luke 7; Matt. 8:1, 5–13; 11:2–30
Oct. 12	Matt. 12:22–50; Mark 3:20–35; Luke 8:1–21
Oct. 13	Mark 4:1–34; Matt. 13:1–53
Oct. 14	Mark 4:35–5:43; Matt. 8:18, 23–34; 9:18–34; Luke 8:22–56
Oct. 15	Mark 6:1–30; Matt. 13:54–58; 9:35–11:1; 14:1–12; Luke 9:1–10
Oct. 16	Matt. 14:13–36; Mark 6:31–56; Luke 9:11–17; John 6:1–21

DATE	TEXT
Oct. 17	John 6:22–7:1; Matt. 15:1–20; Mark 7:1–23
Oct. 18	Matt. 15:21–16:20; Mark 7:24–8:30; Luke 9:18–21
Oct. 19	Matt. 16:21–17:27; Mark 8:31–9:32; Luke 9:22–45
Oct. 20	Matt. 18; 8:19–22; Mark 9:33–50; Luke 9:46–62; John 7:2–10
Oct. 21	John 7:11–8:59
Oct. 22	Luke 10:1–11:36
Oct. 23	Luke 11:37–13:21
Oct. 24	John 9–10
Oct. 25	Luke 13:22–15:32
Oct. 26	Luke 16:1–17:10; John 11:1–54
Oct. 27	Luke 17:11–18:17; Matt. 19:1–15; Mark 10:1–16
Oct. 28	Matt. 19:16–20:28; Mark 10:17–45; Luke 18:18–34
Oct. 29	Matt. 20:29–34; 26:6–13; Mark 10:46–52; 14:3–9; Luke 18:35–19:28; John 11:55–12:11
Oct. 30	Matt. 21:1–22; Mark 11:1–26; Luke 19:29–48; John 12:12–50
Oct. 31	Matt. 21:23–22:14; Mark 11:27–12:12; Luke 20:1–19

Getting to Know . . .

MATTHEW

Author: Matthew

Date: The 50s or 60s A.D.

Background: Matthew, who was surnamed Levi (Mark 2:14), was a Jewish tax collector (publican) for the Roman government. Because he collaborated with the Romans, who were hated by the Jews as overlords of their country, Matthew (and all publicans) was despised by fellow Jews. Nevertheless, Matthew responded to Christ's simple call to follow Him. After the account of the banquet he gave for his colleagues so they, too, could meet Jesus, he is not mentioned again except in the list of the Twelve (Matthew 10:3; see also Acts 1:13).

Overview: Matthew opens with the declaration that Jesus is the "Christ the son of David, the son of Abraham." In fact, eight of the twelve references to Jesus as the son of David are in Matthew, who so clearly pictures Jesus as the ideal Israelite and the ideal King of Israel.

But when Joseph is instructed how to name Jesus, the angel says to name Him Jesus in order to fulfill the prophecy that He would be called "Immanuel" (1:21–23). The key is to understand the name *Jesus* in Hebrew. It is Greek for "Joshua," which means "Yahweh is salvation." He is to be called "Yahweh is salvation" because "he will save his people from their sins."

Matthew opens his gospel with the amazing revelation that Jesus is Yahweh, and Jesus closes it in similar fashion when He says, "And surely *I am with you* always, to the very end of the age" (italics added). That statement was no accidental parallel to Exodus 3:12–15.

MARK

Author: Mark

Date: The 50s or 60s A.D.

Background: It is generally agreed that Mark—while not an apostle himself—received much of the information in his gospel from Peter. Thus, with Peter's apostolic authority behind the gospel, there was never any challenge to its inclusion in the canon of Scripture.

Overview: Perhaps the first gospel account written, Mark opens with: "The beginning of the gospel about Jesus Christ, the Son of God." God Himself ratifies that declaration in 1:11: "You are my Son, whom I love; with you I am well pleased."

By the middle of the book, the disciples have realized the truth of the first half of Jesus' identity, as Peter declares, "You are the Christ" (8:29). But the first to recognize the second half, the divine half, is a centurion. After hearing Jesus' death-cry and observing the way He died, he says, "Surely this man was the Son of God" (15:39). The resurrection that follows proves it to the rest of Jesus' followers, both then and now.

LUKE

Author: Luke

Date: A.D. 60

Background: Luke, the "beloved physician" (Colossians 4:14 KJV), close friend and companion of Paul, was probably the only Gentile author of any part of the New Testament. We know nothing about his early life or conversion except that he was not an eyewitness of the life of Jesus Christ (Luke 1:2). Though a physician by profession, he was primarily an evangelist, writing this gospel and the book of Acts and accompanying Paul in missionary work. He was with Paul at the time of the apostle's martyrdom (2 Timothy 4:11), but of his later life we have no certain facts.

Overview: Like Matthew, Luke proclaims the miraculous, virgin conception of Jesus (1:26–28). He alone writes of the glory of God that was manifested at the birth of Jesus (2:9), an event that was expected to happen only with the coming of the Messiah. Luke also emphasizes the personal encounters with Jesus—Elizabeth and Mary, the shepherds, Simeon and Anna—and shows Jesus identifying throughout His ministry with the lowly, the outcast, and with women. Luke reinforces Jesus' identity with humanity by referring to Him as "son of man" 25 times, second only to Matthew.

JOHN

Author: The apostle John

Date: A.D. 85–90

Background: John the apostle was the son of Zebedee and Salome, and was the younger brother of James. He was a Galilean who apparently came from a fairly well-to-do home (Mark 15:40–41). Though often painted centuries later as effeminate, his real character was such that he was known as a "Son of Thunder" (Mark 3:17). He played a leading role in the work of the early church in Jerusalem (Acts 3:1; 8:14; Galatians 2:9). Later he went to Ephesus, and for an unknown reason was exiled to the island of Patmos (Revelation 1:9).

Overview: We have already seen John's incredible introduction of Jesus as the Word, the Dwelling Presence and the Glory of God. He lists seven self-descriptions of Jesus as "I am" (6:35; 8:12; 9:5; 10:7, 9; 10:11, 14; 11:25; 14:6; 15:1) in addition to his powerful statements in 8:58 and 18:6, the latter demonstrating the power of the name on Jesus' lips.

John refers to Jesus as the "son of man" 13 times, but as "the Son" 20 times. John reveals Jesus as God's unique ("only begotten" KJV) Son, and refers to God as His Father more than any other book of the Bible. The Old Testament refers to God as Father only 12 times, but John does it 120 times!

As you read the gospels chronologically and in harmony, look for their manifold yet unified portrayal of Jesus as *Yahweh* present to save.

Going Deeper . . .

As noted above, the four writers of the Gospels ascribe many names to Jesus. For more on Jesus' names in the Gospels and their relationship to Old Testaments descriptions of Messiah and His sonship, read "The Names and Titles of Jesus" in the back of the book.

Coming up: November and December mark two great Christian celebrations. Believers in the United States give thanks for God's bountiful supply at Thanksgiving. Christians in most countries celebrate Christmas, a time of gift giving and family gatherings to recall God's greatest gift—the coming of His Son, Jesus, to restore men and women to their Creator.

During those busy times of meeting with family and worshiping God, continue to read through the Bible day by day. Be diligent and reach the goal of reading through the Bible in a year! To help you toward the goal, there will be no addional "Going Deeper" articles to read in November and December.

November

Do not merely listen to the word, and so deceive yourselves. Do what it says.
—James 1:22

BIBLE READING SCHEDULE

DATE	TEXT
Nov. 1	Matt. 22:15–46; Mark 12:13–37; Luke 20:20–44
Nov. 2	Matt. 23; Mark 12:38–44; Luke 20:45–21:4
Nov. 3	Matt. 24:1–31; Mark 13:1–27; Luke 21:5–27
Nov. 4	Matt. 24:32–26:5, 14–16; Mark 13:28–14:2, 10–11; Luke 21:28–22:6
Nov. 5	Matt. 26:17–29; Mark 14:12–25; Luke 22:7–38; John 13
Nov. 6	John 14–16
Nov. 7	John 17:1–18:1; Matt. 26:30–46; Mark 14:26–42; Luke 22:39–46
Nov. 8	Matt. 26:47–75; Mark 14:43–72; Luke 22:47–65; John 18:2–27
Nov. 9	Matt. 27:1–26; Mark 15:1–15; Luke 22:66–23:25; John 18:28–19:16
Nov. 10	Matt. 27:27–56; Mark 15:16–41; Luke 23:26–49; John 19:17–30
Nov. 11	Matt. 27:57–28:8; Mark 15:42–16:8; Luke 23:50–24:12; John 19:31–20:10

DATE	TEXT
Nov. 12	Matt. 28:9–20; Mark 16:9–20; Luke 24:13–53; John 20:11–21:25
Nov. 13	Acts 1–2
Nov. 14	Acts 3–5
Nov. 15	Acts 6:1–8:1
Nov. 16	Acts 8:3–9:43
Nov. 17	Acts 10–11
Nov. 18	Acts 12–13
Nov. 19	Acts 14–15
Nov. 20	Gal. 1–3
Nov. 21	Gal. 4–6
Nov. 22	James
Nov. 23	Acts 16:1–18:11
Nov. 24	1 Thessalonians
Nov. 25	2 Thessalonians; Acts 18:12–19:22
Nov. 26	1 Cor. 1–4
Nov. 27	1 Cor. 5–8
Nov. 28	1 Cor. 9–11
Nov. 29	1 Cor. 12–14
Nov. 30	1 Cor. 15–16

Getting to Know . . .

ACTS

Author: Luke

Date: A.D. 61

Theme: The Acts of the Apostles gives us the record of the spread of Christianity from the coming of the Spirit on the day of Pentecost to Paul's arrival in Rome to preach the gospel in the world's capital. In this regard, then, it is the record of the continuation of those things that Jesus began while on earth, and that He continued as the risen head of the church and the One who sent the Holy Spirit.

Overview: The book traditionally known as the The Acts of the Apostles could well be titled "The Acts of the Spirit," for it begins with the Spirit's promised coming and moves to its conclusion by presenting His power, filling, and direction. So as you read Acts, look behind the well-known personalities of Peter, Stephen, Philip, Barnabas, Silas, and Paul to the Spirit that transformed them into amazing men of God.

Also important to note is that God's character does not change, but His ways of interacting with creation do. Just because something occurred in biblical history does not mean it should happen all the time. For example, you do not have to go and "tarry in Jerusalem" to receive the Spirit—He meets you where you are. What is portrayed in Acts truly happened, but our patterns today for living in the Spirit are better taken from the epistles.

The Epistles

As we read the history of the early church in Acts, we encounter the epistles, or letters, in which the apostles send instructions, answer questions, and counter false teaching in the young local churches. Some of those instructions and commands are bound to time and culture. For example, don't bother to go to Troas to fetch Paul's cloak, though that is commanded in 2 Timothy 4:13. But most of what was written 1,900 years ago applies to us today.

As you read these letters, read them personally. Rather than being overwhelmed by their hundreds of concepts and commands, find one thing each day to use in your worship and apply to your life.

GALATIANS

Author: Paul

Date: A.D. 49 or 55

Background: At the time of the writing of this letter, the term *Galatia* was used both in a geographical and in a political sense. The former referred to north-central Asia Minor, north of the cities of Pisidian, Antioch, Iconium,

Lystra, and Derbe; the latter referred to the Roman province (organized in 25 B.C.) that included southern districts and those cities just mentioned. If the letter was written to Christians in northern Galatia, the churches were founded on the second missionary journey and the epistle was written on the third missionary journey. If the letter was written to Christians in southern Galatia, the churches were founded on the first missionary journey, and the letter was written after the end of that journey (probably from Antioch, circa A.D. 49, making it the earliest of Paul's epistles).

Overview: Perhaps the first letter of Paul—maybe even of the whole New Testament—Galatians was written about A.D. 49 to counter false teaching about Christianity and the law and the relationship between faith and works. Just as God saves us without our work, likewise our growth and holiness comes not by our works, but by dependence on the power of God's indwelling Spirit.

JAMES

Author: James
Date: A.D. 45–50
Background: James, along with 1 and 2 Peter; 1, 2, and 3 John; and Jude, were called the "general," "universal," or "catholic" epistles by the early church because their addresses (with the exception of 2 and 3 John) were not limited to a single locality. James, for example, is addressed "to the twelve tribes scattered among the nations" (1:1)—a designation for believers everywhere (which were likely all Jewish Christians at that early date).

Overview: Some read James as a counter to Paul when he says, "Faith by itself, if it is not accompanied by action, is dead" (2:17). But far from contradicting Paul, James was talking about lifestyle. He draws from a rich heritage of wisdom, the prophets, and his half-brother's Sermon on the Mount to write about the life of faith that *looks* theologically correct.

THESSALONIANS

Author: Paul
Date: Both 1 and 2 Thessalonians were written in A.D. 51.
Background: Paul, Silas, and Timothy first went to the Macedonian port city of Thessalonica on their second missionary journey (Acts 17:1–14). This was the second place the gospel was preached in Europe, with Philippi being the first.

Overview: Addressed to one of Paul's first churches in Greece, 1 and 2 Thessalonians encourage the young believers to endure persecution, resist false teaching, and live full and productive lives as they await Christ's certain return. In fact, each of 1 Thessalonians' five chapters ends with encouragement based on the second coming.

CORINTHIANS

Author: Paul

Date: 1 Corinthians was written in A.D. 55. 2 Corinthians was written in A.D. 56.

Background: The gospel was first preached in Corinth by Paul on his second missionary journey (A.D. 50). Paul remained 18 months in the city (Acts 18:1–17; 1 Cor. 2:3). After leaving, Paul wrote the church a letter, which has been lost (1 Cor. 5:9), but disturbing news about the believers and questions they asked Paul in a letter they sent to him (7:1) prompted the writing of 1 Corinthians. Later the apostle found it necessary to make a hurried visit to the city, as the problems cited in the first letter had not been resolved (2 Cor. 2:1; 12:14; 13:1–2). The second letter was written from Macedonia, and Paul followed it with his final recorded visit to the church (Acts 20:1–4).

Overview: At Corinth, Paul spent one-and-one-half years developing the church. His longest letters and most impassioned correspondence were to those troubled believers. Their affluent and fast-growing port town brought them an inordinate amount of contact with immorality, pagan religion, and philosophy. Their problems with arrogance, leader-worshiping cliques, immorality, divorce, and misunderstandings of spiritual gifts are systematically addressed in response to their questions.

December

And I heard a loud voice from the throne saying, "Now the dwelling of God is with men, and he will live with them. They will be his people, and God himself will be with them and be their God. He will wipe every tear from their eyes. There will be no more death or mourning or crying or pain, for the old order of things has passed away."
—Revelation 21:3–4

BIBLE READING SCHEDULE

DATE	TEXT	DATE	TEXT
Dec. 1	Acts 19:23–20:1; 2 Cor. 1–4	**Dec. 17**	Philemon; 1 Tim. 1–3
Dec. 2	2 Cor. 5–9	**Dec. 18**	1 Tim. 4–6; Titus
Dec. 3	2 Cor. 10–13	**Dec. 19**	2 Timothy
Dec. 4	Rom. 1–3	**Dec. 20**	1 Peter
Dec. 5	Rom. 4–6	**Dec. 21**	Jude; 2 Peter
Dec. 6	Rom. 7–8	**Dec. 22**	Heb. 1:1–5:10
Dec. 7	Romans 9–11	**Dec. 23**	Heb. 5:11–9:28
Dec. 8	Romans 12–15	**Dec. 24**	Heb. 10–11
Dec. 9	Romans 16; Acts 20:2–21:16	**Dec. 25**	Heb. 12–13; 2 John; 3 John
Dec. 10	Acts 21:17–23:35	**Dec. 26**	1 John
Dec. 11	Acts 24–26	**Dec. 27**	Rev. 1–3
Dec. 12	Acts 27–28	**Dec. 28**	Rev. 4–9
Dec. 13	Eph. 1–3	**Dec. 29**	Rev. 10–14
Dec. 14	Eph. 4–6	**Dec. 30**	Rev. 15–18
Dec. 15	Colossians	**Dec. 31**	Rev. 19–22
Dec. 16	Philippians		

Getting to Know . . .

ROMANS

Author: Paul the apostle
Date: A.D. 57–58
Background: Though both Paul and Peter were apparently martyred in Rome, it is unlikely that either was the founder of the church in that city. Possibly some who were converted on the day of Pentecost (Acts 2:10) carried the gospel back to the imperial city; or it may be that converts of Paul or of other apostles founded the church there. We do know that the membership was predominantly Gentile (1:13; 11:13; 15:15–16).
Overview: Paul's letter to Rome is better known in the church than any other. Its systematic presentation of major theological themes is foundational for understanding the nature of the Christian faith, the righteousness of God, salvation, and the roles of Israel and the church. And because Paul was not acquainted with the church at Rome, the letter is less personal and culture-bound than his others; thus it appears more universally and directly applicable to the church through the ages.

Read Romans as if for the first time and look for its unique revelation of God's attributes and actions. You will be powerfully impressed by God's righteousness, just wrath, unfailing love, absolute faithfulness, awesome sovereignty, and unique wisdom—not to mention His incredible gift of life.

EPHESIANS

Author: Paul
Date: A.D. 61
Background: Christianity probably came first to Ephesus with Aquila and Priscilla when Paul made a brief stop there on his second missionary journey (Acts 18:18–19). On his third journey, he stayed in the city for about three years, and the gospel spread throughout Asia Minor (Acts 19:10). The city was a commercial, political, and religious center because of the great temple of Artemis. After Paul, Timothy had charge of the church in Ephesus for a time (1 Timothy 1:3), and later the apostle John made the city his headquarters.
Overview: Shortly after Paul returned to Jerusalem from his third missionary journey, he was arrested in the temple courtyard, imprisoned in Caesarea for two years, and tried by Felix and Festus. He then appealed to Agrippa to be sent to Rome for trial before Caesar. Though Agrippa comments to Festus that Paul might have been freed except for that appeal (Acts 26:32), Scripture indicates it was clearly in God's plan to send him to the empire's capital, as yet untouched by the apostles.

While under house arrest in rented quarters in Rome, Paul wrote four letters known as the prison epistles. Of those, Ephesians is the best known for its tremendous theological content, which seems to drift in long, flowing statements of praise for God's work in Christ. Paul makes clear that as God is one, the church must be one. Although there are a diversity of gifts—and although Paul addresses husbands, wives, children, slaves, and masters separately—he emphasizes that all are one in Christ.

COLOSSIANS
Author: Paul
Date: A.D. 61
Background: About one hundred miles east of Ephesus, and near Laodicea and Hierapolis (4:13), Colossae was an ancient but declining commercial center. The gospel may have been taken there during Paul's ministry at Ephesus (Acts 19:10), though it was Epaphras who played the major role in the evangelism and growth of the Colossians. Paul was personally unacquainted with the believers there (2:1), but Epaphras either visited Paul in prison or was imprisoned with him (Philemon 23) and reported on conditions in this church.
Overview: The book of Colossians has much in common with Ephesians and was probably written at the same time. Unique to Colossians, however, is Paul's attack against a local heresy that depreciated the person of Christ and promoted ritualism; asceticism; and special, hidden knowledge. To counter that, Paul praises Jesus as the center and substance of the universe.

PHILEMON
Author: Paul
Date: A.D. 63
Background: Like Ephesians, Philippians, and Colossians, Philemon is one of the Prison Epistles, written during Paul's first confinement in Rome. Onesimus, one of the millions of slaves in the Roman Empire, had stolen from his master, Philemon, and had run away.
Overview: Philemon is one of the shortest New Testament letters. Addressed to a member of the Colossian church, Philemon, Paul encouraged him to act more like a Christian than a Roman in accepting back his runaway slave, Onesimus. Luther compared Paul's reconciliation of this slave and master to Christ's reconciliation of the believer with God the Father.

PHILIPPIANS
Author: Paul
Date: A.D. 63
Background: Paul began the church at Philippi during his second missionary journey, and it was the first church to be established in Europe (Acts

16). Philippi was a small city that had been founded by King Philip of Macedonia, father of Alexander the Great. Its greatest fame came from the battle fought nearby, in 42 B.C., between the forces of Brutus and Cassius and those of Antony and Octavian (later known as Caesar Augustus).

Overview: Paul and Silas visited Philippi, their first Macedonian contact, on their second missionary journey in A.D. 52. To the saints and leadership of the church, Paul wrote of joyful submission to the will of God, regardless of circumstances, and used the awe-inspiring example of Christ Jesus as the model of humility and mutual submission within the church.

TIMOTHY AND TITUS

Author: Paul

Dates: 1 Timothy and Titus were written between A.D. 63 and 66. 2 Timothy was written in A.D. 67.

Background: Timothy, the son of a Greek Gentile father and a devout Jewish mother named Eunice, was intimately associated with Paul from the time of the second missionary journey on (2 Timothy 1:5; Acts 16:1–3). Titus was a Gentile by birth and was converted through the ministry of Paul (Titus 1:4). He accompanied Paul to Jerusalem at the time of the apostolic council (Acts 15:2; Galatians 2:1–3). He was also Paul's emissary to the church at Corinth during the third missionary journey (2 Cor. 7:6–7; 8:6, 16).

Overview: Timothy and Titus were two special disciples in whom Paul invested much time, and to whom he entrusted great responsibility. His letters to them are usually dated after the events of Acts 28; tradition tells us Paul was then released from prison and that he embarked on further missionary ventures from A.D. 62 to 67, until his final imprisonment, trial, and execution.

Addressing Timothy as his envoy to Ephesus, Paul instructs him in his personal ministry in the affairs of worship, women, widows, and wealth, and in the appointment of qualified leaders to carry on the ministry. Considered Paul's last letter, 2 Timothy reveals Paul's concern for Timothy's continuing faithfulness to his calling, his struggle against false teachers, and his fidelity to the apostolic tradition based on the inspired Word of God.

Timothy was especially dear to Paul, but Titus was his troubleshooter. When Paul's authority was challenged in Corinth, Paul sent Titus to straighten out matters (2 Cor. 2:13; 7:6–14). Titus was also sent to deal with the "liars, evil brutes, lazy gluttons" on Crete (Titus 1:12). Much of Titus parallels 1 Timothy, but is less personal and more compact.

PETER AND JUDE

Authors: Peter and Jude

Dates: The epistle 1 Peter was written between A.D. 63 and 64; 2 Peter was written in 66. Jude was written between 70 and 80.

Background: Peter wrote his letters to "strangers . . . scattered"—or literally, the "sojourners of the dispersion" (1 Peter 1:1). These were Christians who, like Israel of old, were scattered throughout the world, though the readers of this epistle were predominantly of Gentile rather than Jewish background. Jude identifies himself as the brother of James (v. 1), the leader of the Jerusalem church (Acts 15), and the half brother of the Lord Jesus (see Matthew 13:55; Mark 6:3). Although, by his own statement, he intended to write a treatise on salvation, pressing circumstances required him to deal instead with false teachers (v. 3).

Overview: First Peter encourages all Christians to live holy and faithful lives, and to be willing to suffer unjust persecution after the example of Christ. Peter challenges wives, husbands, elders, and young men to exercise humility, service, and self-control.

Second Peter and Jude are so alike that many have wondered why both are needed in the New Testament. But slight variances in content and emphases are unique and merit careful study. Both deal urgently with an insidious and dangerous heresy that threatens the very lives of believers. Peter says the key to stability and growth is knowing God (2 Peter 1:5–11).

HEBREWS

Author: Uncertain

Date: A.D. 64–68

Background: Many suggestions have been made for the author of this anonymous book—Paul, Barnabas, Apollos, Silas, Aquila and Priscilla, and Clement of Rome. There are both resemblances and dissimilarities to the theology and style of Paul, but Paul frequently appeals to his own apostolic authority in his letters, while this writer appeals to others who were eyewitnesses of Jesus' ministry (2:3). It's safest to say, as did the theologian Origen in the third century, that only God knows who wrote Hebrews.

Overview: We cannot be sure who wrote Hebrews. But the anonymity of the author does not detract from the letter's authority. Hebrews speaks powerfully of the superiority of Christ, exalting Him over the angels (1–2), Moses (3–4) and the Aaronic priesthood (5–7), as well as the superiority of Christ's new covenant and sacrifice over the old (8–10). Chapters 11 to 13 plead for lives of faith in light of Christ's work and examples from the faithful of old.

LETTERS OF JOHN

Author: John the apostle

Date: 1, 2, and 3 John were all written in A.D. 90.

Background: Strong tradition says that John spent his old age in Ephesus, and that these letters were written after the completion of his Gospel, but before his persecution under Domitian in A.D. 95.

Overview: Reading the letters of John is almost like reading a personalized synopsis of his gospel, but with the life-related concerns of James. John encourages believers to emulate God's love, as shown in His Son, by individually and sacrificially meeting personal needs. He also commands his readers to reject the world in order to love the Father, and to reject false teachers and false (anti-) christs by recalling the apostles' teaching and the witness of the Spirit.

REVELATION

Author: John the apostle

Date: A.D. 90s

Background: This book was clearly written in a period of time when Christians were threatened by Rome, undoubtedly by pressure to make them recant their faith and accept the cult of emperor worship. Some maintain that the book was written during Nero's persecution of Christians after the burning of Rome in A.D. 64. However, the more probable date is during the harsh reign of that warped personality Domitian (A.D. 81–96).

Overview: Revelation is perhaps the most abused book in Scripture. For generations this book has been read as a timetable for the end times. More important, however, is its revelation of the character of the Lamb and the sovereignty of God, both of which should encourage believers of all ages—not just the last—to "overcome the world" with their faith and faithfulness toward God.

Revelation contains more hymns of praise—more words of adoration to the Lamb, the Father, and the Spirit—than any other New Testament book. Rather than try to identify the dragon and his beasts, adore the true Trinity, who is sovereign over space and time.

Going Deeper

THE PRIMARY NAMES OF GOD

In the ancient Near East, one's name provided a key to his or her character. Adam was named for the ground (*adamah*) from which he was formed (Genesis 2:7). Eve, as the mother of all people, was named "Living" (*havvah*; Genesis 3:20). The fool who refused hospitality to David and his men in 1 Samuel 25 was appropriately named Nabal, or "Fool."

In the Old Testament, three terms are generally considered the primary names of God. In our English versions, they usually appear as "God," "Lord," and "LORD." Each name has a meaning all its own. The word *God* is usually translated as one of three related Hebrew words—*El*, *Eloah*, and *Elohim*—which have the basic meaning of "might" or "strength." So they describe deity as "the Mighty One." It is no wonder that *Elohim* is used 35 times in Genesis 1:1—2:3 to describe the God who created the universe.

These words assume the existence of God and describe His power (Romans 1:20), but they convey nothing unique about the God of the Bible. In fact, the Bible and other ancient texts use *El*, *Eloah*, and *Elohim* to describe other gods (Genesis 31:30-32) or even mighty people (Exodus 22:8-9; "judges"). But what is unique to biblical usage is the plural word *Elohim*, referring to one God.

The use of the plural to address one individual is not uncommon in ancient texts; it is called the "plural of majesty" or "respect." But there may be a hint of the Trinity when this form is used in the Bible. It occurs at least 2,340 times as a name of God in the text, compared to about 205 times for *El* and 50 times for *Eloah*, both singular forms.

The word *Lord* occurs nearly 640 times in the New Testament (as a title for Jesus or the Father), but only about 460 times in the Old. Like the words for God, the Hebrew word *Adon* can refer to lords or masters other than the Lord of all creation (Genesis 42:30, 33). But like *Elohim*, the plural form *Adonay* is the normal form of this word when referring to *the* Lord. Furthermore, the "ay" at the end of this Hebrew word includes the personal pronoun *my*. In other words, the term could be translated as "my Lord," especially when the relationship of Sovereign Master to submissive servant is clear from the text (Genesis 15:2, 8).

The word *Loi* outnumbers the combined total of all other names and titles of God, occurring more than 6,800 times. Unlike these other words, it is the unique proper name of the one true God—the name He shares with no other. Most scholars believe this name was originally pronounced "Yahweh."

Yahweh is the name by which God relates to His people. It's the name that implies His presence and interaction. Thus, though God, "the Mighty One," created the universe in Genesis 1, *Yahweh* stooped down to form man from the dust and to breathe life into his nostrils.

Here are the common names of God found in Genesis and Job, the earliest books of the biblical chronology:

Book	Elohim "God"	El "God"	Adonay "Lord"/"lord"	Elyon "Most High"	Shaddai "Almighty"	Yahweh "LORD"
Genesis	213/4*	19	9/2#	4	6	165
Job	57 /1*	56	1	1	31	32

*El or Elohim when used of a "god" other than the true God have an asterisk (*).

#Adon, "lord," and Elohim, "gods," when used of human authority, have a pound sign (#).

TEN STRATEGIES FOR FIRST-RATE READING: PART 1

As readers of the Bible, we're often required to assume the role of a biblical detective, searching for clues as to the meaning of the text. But as any detective will tell you, there is more than one way to crack a case.

Sherlock Holmes, the master sleuth, can sometimes be found on his hands and knees, inspecting the floor for cigar ashes or footprints. Other times he broods for hours, rolling things over and over in his mind, straining for answers. He assumes disguises, feigns sickness, conducts experiments—whatever it takes to solve the mystery.

In the same way, finding clues in the biblical text demands more than one approach. The Bible must be read to be understood. But there is more than one way to read it. In fact, I'm going to give you ten strategies that can turn you into a first-rate reader. Each one yields different clues about what the text means.

1. Read Thoughtfully

Thoughtful reading involves study. Not boredom. Far from it. When you come to the Bible, put your thinking cap on. Don't throw your mind into neutral. Apply the same mental discipline that you would to any subject in which you take a vital interest. Are you a stockbroker? Then use the same mental intensity to study Scripture that you would the *Wall Street Journal.* Are you a pilot? Then pay as much attention to the Word as you would to a flight plan or a weather advisory. Are you a nurse? Then look for the "vital signs" in the biblical text just as you would with any patient on your floor. The Bible does not yield its fruit to the lazy.

Proverbs 2:4 gives an interesting insight concerning the richness of God's Word. It admonishes us to "seek [wisdom] as silver, and search for her as for hidden treasures" (NASB). In other words, biblical wisdom is like precious ore. It's not found lying around on the surface, but at a deeper level. A good analogy for our own day would be the many oil deposits under the parched deserts of the Middle East. For millennia, people wandered across those trackless wastes, unaware that only a few thousand feet away lay resources of unimaginable value.

So it is with Scripture. The very truth of God is there, able to transform your life. But you must probe for it. You've got to penetrate the surface with more than just a cursory glance. In other words, you've got to think.

2. Read Repeatedly

Years ago I read a book about the Bible in which the author wrote, "When I read this passage for the one hundredth time, the following idea came to me. . . ." I thought, *You've got to be kidding!* In those days, if I read a portion of Scripture twice, it would be incredible. If I read it three or four times, it would be miraculous. But here was this great, seasoned student of Scripture telling me that I needed to read it over and over again—not once or twice, but a hundred times, if necessary, to gain insight.

Today I realize that he was wisely practicing the second strategy to first-rate Bible reading.

The genius of the Word of God is that it has staying power; it can stand up to repeated exposure. In fact, that's why it is unlike any other book. You may be an expert in a given field. So if you read a book in that field two or three times, you've got it. You can put it on the shelf and move on to something else.

But that's never true of the Bible. Read it over and over again, and you'll still see things that you've never seen before.

3. Read Patiently

There's an old saying that nothing good happens fast. I don't know if that's altogether true, but it does have some bearing on Bible study. Unless you've got highly developed habits of reading, it is unlikely that you can just dip into the Word for five minutes and come away with much of significance. In fact, highly skilled readers devote a lot more than five minutes to the task.

They've learned to approach Scripture using the third strategy of first-rate reading: Read patiently.

That's a hard assignment for most of us. We live in an instant society. The things we used to want tomorrow, we now want right now. And the things we used to need right away, we now need yesterday. So it's no surprise that if we decide to open our Bibles, we expect results instantly and effort-lessly. If we don't hit the jackpot in short order, we're liable to get very frus-trated, very quickly.

But the fruit of the Word takes time to ripen. So if you are the least bit impatient, you're liable to bail out early and miss a rich harvest. Many peo-ple do that. They get disillusioned with the process. Perhaps they are look-ing for entertainment rather than enlightenment. People tell me, "Look, I tried to read the Bible, but it's like plowing through concrete."

Others give up on the biblical text and turn instead to secondary sources. The moment they think they are in over their heads, they make a mad dash for a commentary to find out what some other significant saint has to say about the passage. In the process, they ruin the experience. In my judgment, people who do that quit too soon. They are usually right on the verge of pay dirt when they go to secondary sources. Don't get me wrong, there's noth-ing wrong with the use of secondary sources—after you have drenched your mind with what the biblical text says.

TEN STRATEGIES FOR
FIRST-RATE READING: PART 2

My sons will tell you that I'm not much of a fisherman. I love to fish, but I don't catch very much. Our family used to take vacations in Col-orado, and we'd go to a little pond where there were trout about half the size of a canoe. But do you think I could hook one of those babies?

I tried every gimmick the tackle shops had to sell. No luck. Those fish would come right up to the shore, and I dangled the hook right in front of their noses. But all in all, I caught very little. The frustrating thing was, just down the shoreline were always a couple of old duffers with two or three rigs, and they couldn't reel the fish in fast enough. We'd be talking to them while they were pulling one in, and meanwhile one of their other lines would be dancing with a strike.

What was their secret? Not only did they know the pond, and not only did they know trout, they knew what bait to use. They illustrate the fourth strategy of first-rate Bible reading.

4. Read Selectively

Meaningful Bible reading includes reading the Scriptures selectively. Con-tinuing our illustration, selective Bible reading means using the right bait when you troll the Scriptures. Here are six "lures" that you can use with any text—six questions to ask any passage of Scripture:

- *Who?* Who are the people in the text? That's a pretty simple question to answer. Just read the text. But once you've identified who is in the passage, I suggest you look for two more things: 1) What is said about the person, and 2) What does the person say?
- *What?* A second question to ask is, What is happening in this text? What are the events? In what order? What happens to the characters? Or, if it's a passage that argues a point: What is the argument; what is the writer trying to communicate?
- *Where?* This gives you the location. Where is the narrative taking place? Where are the people in the story? Where are they coming from? Where are they going? Where is the writer? Where were the original readers of this text? The question "Where?" is one reason to have a set of maps or an atlas nearby whenever you study the Bible
- *When?* This is the question of time. When did the events in the text take place? When did they occur in relation to other events in Scripture? When was the writer writing? In short, always determine what time it is.
- *Why?* There is an infinity of "Why?" questions to ask the biblical text. Why is this included? Why is it placed here? Why does this follow that? Why does this precede that? Why does this person say that? Why does that person say nothing? "Why?" is a question that digs for meaning.
- *Wherefore?* I like to paraphrase this question as, "So what?" What difference would it make if I were to apply this truth? "Wherefore?" is the question that gets us started doing something about what we've read. Remember, the Word of God was not written to satisfy our curiosity; it was written to change our lives. So with any passage of Scripture, we need to ask, "So what?"

5. Read Prayerfully

We tend to think of Bible study and prayer as separate disciplines, but the fact is, they are integrally related. Prayer is really a key to effective Bible study. So learn to pray before, during, and after your reading of the Scriptures.

Prayer is especially crucial when you come to a place in your study where you are stuck and confused. That's a good time to stop and carry on a conversation with God. "Lord, I can't make any sense out of this passage. I don't understand it. Give me insight. Help me to discover Your truth."

6. Read Imaginatively

It is sad but true that the average person thinks that reading the Bible is dreadfully boring. In fact, the only thing more boring would be listening to someone teach from the Bible. Yet I'm convinced that the reason Scripture seems dull to so many people is that we come to it dully.

How different things would be if we employed the sixth strategy for first-rate Bible reading: Read imaginatively.

Often when we come to the Scriptures, we use the least imaginative, most overworked approaches possible. For instance, in a small group Bible study, the leader has each person read a verse aloud. Unfortunately, the first guy is not such a good reader. Then the second person has one of those exotic modern translations, and no one else can follow along. Catastrophe strikes when the next person reads verse 3—it's verse 3 in a different book of the Bible. And so it goes. By the time it's over, nobody has the foggiest idea what the passage really says.

By contrast, our church used to have a pastor who was a master at dramatic presentations of Scripture. He had a background in theater, and he used it to his advantage. Frequently he assumed the role of a biblical character in front of the congregation. He put on makeup and a costume. He did all kinds of background studies to give us a feel for the cultural setting. And then he told the character's story in the first person, using simple, everyday language. As a result, by the time he finished, we were not simply entertained, we were instructed. Our imaginations kicked into gear, and we entered into the text. We understood how biblical truth and human experience could mingle.

One of the things I'd love to see more people do when they study the Bible is to pray this simple prayer: "Lord, clothe the facts with fascination. Help me crawl into the skin of these people—to see through their eyes, to feel with their fingers, to understand with their hearts, and to know with their minds." Then the Word of God would become alive

TEN STRATEGIES FOR
FIRST-RATE READING: PART 3

Here are some final strategies to enhance your reading and understanding of the Bible.

7. Read Meditatively

The seventh strategy to becoming a first-rate reader of the Bible is a hard one for most of us: Read meditatively. In other words, learn to reflect on what you read in the Bible. That's hard, because more and more of us are living in the "laser lane." In the old days, if people missed the stagecoach, they'd say, "That's OK. We'll catch it next month." Today, if a guy misses a section of a revolving door, it throws him into a tizzy!

As a result, meditative Bible reading has fallen out of favor. As I said earlier, we live in an instant society—a distracted society. We've got so much stuff coming at us from TV, cell phones, e-mail, snail mail, BlackBerries, satellite links, cable feeds, and podcasts that we barely have time to react, never mind reflect.

But you can't "download" spirituality. And that's why Scripture speaks so frequently about meditation.

When you read meditatively, the goal is to chew on the Word, looking for insights, and to examine yourself, looking for ways to apply Scripture. Be sure to write down everything you observe in the passage, as well as your conclusions. And spend time in prayer. On the basis of what you've studied and meditated on, what is God telling you? What do you need to tell Him? Where do you need His resources and help? What opportunities for evangelism would you like Him to open for you?

8. Read Purposefully

Paul explained in 2 Timothy 3:16–17 says that all Scripture is given by divine inspiration and is "profitable." In other words, it serves a purpose—four purposes, as a matter of fact: teaching, reproof, correction, and instruction in righteous living. This suggests an eighth strategy for first-rate reading of Scripture: Reading purposefully.

Purposeful reading looks for the aim of the author. There isn't a verse of Scripture that was thrown in by accident. Every word contributes to meaning. Your challenge as a reader is to discern that meaning.

9. Read Acquisitively

To read the Bible acquisitively means that we read not only to receive the Word from God, but to retain it. We don't read merely to perceive something, but to possess it—to stake a claim on the text and make it our own property.

How can that happen? The key is personal, active involvement in the process. There's an old proverb to that effect: "I hear, and I forget. I see, and I remember. I do, and I understand." Modern psychological studies back that up with scientific data. We remember at most only 10 percent of what we hear; 50 percent of what we see and hear; but 90 percent of what we see, hear, and do.

Still not sure what it means to read acquisitively? Then I suggest you give it a try right here and now. Turn to Numbers 13, the story of the spies sent by Moses into the Promised Land. Read the account carefully, using all of the principles we've covered so far. Then write your own paraphrase of the story.

Here are a few suggestions:

1. Decide what the main point of the story is. What happens? Why is this incident significant?
2. Think about any parallels to what happens here in the history of your own family, church, or nation, or in your own life.
3. Decide on the "angle" you want to use. For instance: the report of a task force for Israel, Inc. (a business angle); a tribal council (a Native American angle); a political contest between two factions (a political or governmental angle). The point is, choose something that fits the situation and will make this incident memorable for you.
4. Rewrite the story according to the angle you have chosen. Use language that fits that motif. Make the characters sound real-to-life. Change names and places to fit the style.
5. When you're finished, read your paraphrase to a friend or someone in your family.

10. Read Telescopically

Telescopic reading means viewing the parts in light of the whole. The Bible is an integrated message in which the whole is greater than the sum of its parts. That's bad math, but good method. And yet what happens in a lot of Bible study and Bible teaching is that we keep breaking it down and breaking it down, until we have nothing left but baskets of fragments. What we need today are people who can put the parts back together again into a meaningful and powerful whole.

So every time you read and analyze Scripture, every time you take it apart, realize that you've only done part of the task. Your next task is to put it back together again.

Judges is a good book with which to try this message. It covers the period in Israel's history just after Joshua's death, but before Israel had a king. God raised up individual leaders, called judges, to lead the people as they settled in the Promised Land.

To gain the broad perspective, read the entire book at one sitting and make a list of who the major characters are—the judges—and where they start appearing in the text. (A key phrase "Then the sons of Israel did evil in the sight of the Lord.") Next, create a chart that shows where each one appears in the book and how much space is given to him or her.

When you complete this exercise, you'll have an excellent start on reading the Book of Judges telescopically. You'll have the big picture so that when you read the stories of the individual judges, you'll have a context in which to place them. Some other Old Testament books I advise reading this way are 1 and 2 Samuel, 1 and 2 Kings, and 1 and 2 Chronicles.

A Proven Method for Studying the Bible

Studying the Bible requires a certain method. That is, it involves taking certain steps in a certain order to guarantee a certain result. Not just any steps; not just any order; not just any result.

And the result governs everything. What is the product of Bible study? What are you after? Personal Bible study should have a very specific aim— namely, life change. So how will you get there? What process will lead to that result? I propose a three-step approach that will guarantee life change—three crucial steps carried out in a particular order.

1. *Observation.* In this step, you ask and answer the question, *What do I see?* The moment you come to the Scriptures, you ask, "What are the facts?" You assume the role of a biblical detective, looking for clues. No detail is trivial. This leads us to the second step . . .

2. *Interpretation.* Here you ask and answer the question, *What does it mean?* Your central quest is for meaning. Unfortunately, too much Bible study begins with interpretation, and, furthermore, it usually ends there. But I'm going to show you that it does not begin there. Before you understand, you have to learn to see. Nor does it end there, because the third step is . . .

3. *Application.* Here you ask and answer the question, *How does it work?* Not, *Does it work?* People say they're going to make the Bible "relevant." But if the Bible is not already relevant, nothing you or I do will help. The Bible is relevant because it is revealed. It's always a return to reality. And for those who read it and heed it, it changes their lives.

Now you know a proven method for studying the Bible. The next step is to open up the Word and do it. Why not right now? And to help you make the most of the experience, here are three habits you can cultivate to increase your productivity. As you'll notice, these habits correspond to the three steps I mentioned above. Use them every time you open your Bible.

1. *Read.* This may seem obvious. Yet too many "readers" are nothing but browsers. They turn pages the way they flip through channels on a TV set, looking for something to catch their interest. The Word doesn't

lend itself to that sort of approach. It requires conscious, concentrated effort. So read portions of the Bible over and over. The more you read them, the more clear they will become. (To learn more, review the article "Ten Strategies for First-Rate Reading.")

2. *Record.* In other words, write some notes. Jot down what you see in the text. Keep a record of your insights and questions. Start where you are, even with very elementary things; be sure to write them down. Use a legal pad or a notebook to record what you see. In your own words, summarize your observations and insights so that later they will come back to you. Doing so will help you remember what you've discovered and use it.

3. *Reflect.* Take some time to think about what you've seen. Ask yourself: What's going on in this passage? What is it telling me about God? About myself? What do I need to do on the basis of what I'm reading here? Simply put, reflection (or meditation) is vital to understanding and applying God's Word.

WHAT TYPE OF LITERATURE IS THIS?: PART 1

In *A Preface to Paradise Lost*, C. S. Lewis writes: "The first qualification for judging any piece of workmanship, from a corkscrew to a cathedral, is to know what it is—what it was intended to do and how it is meant to be used. . . . The first thing the reader needs to know about *Paradise Lost* is what Milton meant it to be."[1]

The same could be said for the Word of God. Before ever launching into a study of a book in the Bible, the first thing a reader needs to know is what that book's author meant it to be. In other words, what kind of literature was he writing? What literary form did he employ?

Believe it or not, the literary genre of a text is crucial to interpretation. Suppose I randomly pick verse from the Scripture: "If only you would slay the wicked, O God" (Ps. 139:19 NASB). Or, "Father Abraham, have mercy on me, and send Lazarus" (Luke 16:24 NASB). Or, "After these things I looked, and behold, a door standing open in heaven" (Revelation 4:1). Unless you know what types of literature those are taken from, you are in no position to determine their meaning.

There are six different kinds of writing that appear in the Bible, and they all influence our understanding of what we read. Please note: This is merely an introduction. We're barely going to scratch the surface on the subject of literary form, which is utterly fascinating.

There are different styles of Scripture—all God-breathed, to be sure, but distinctive in terms of literary form. The more you understand about a given form, the better you'll be able to interpret Scripture.

Here, then, are the first five of the major literary genres that God used to communicate His message.

Exposition

An exposition is a straightforward argument or explanation of a body of objective truth. It is a form of writing that appeals primarily to the mind. The argument usually has a tight structure that moves from point to point in logical fashion.

Paul's letters are outstanding examples of the expositional form in Scripture. The letter to the Romans is a tightly reasoned explanation of the gospel. Paul argues like a lawyer presenting a case before a court, which is no surprise because we know that as a young man Paul had extensive rabbinical training, including the oratorical arts.

Expositional books are ideal if you're just getting started in Bible study. Their meaning lies close to the surface. They appeal to the average person's preference for logic, structure, and order. And their purposes are easy to grasp; they practically outline themselves. Yet they also make for exciting in-depth analysis because their truths are inexhaustible.

The key to understanding a work of exposition is to pay attention to its structure and the terms it employs.

Narrative and Biography

Narrative means story. The Bible is full of stories, which is one reason it is so popular.

For example, Genesis relates the story of God's creation of the world, the story of the flood, the story of the tower at Babel, and the story of the patriarchs (Abraham, Isaac, Jacob, and Joseph). Exodus continues the story by recounting Israel's departure from Egypt, led by Moses. Ruth tells the story of Ruth, the great-grandmother of King David.

In the New Testament, the four Gospels tell the story of Jesus from four different points of view. One of them, Luke, continues the narrative in the Acts of the Apostles. Within the accounts of Jesus, we find stories that He told to His followers.

So the Bible is heavily composed of stories. That makes for interesting reading, but it also makes or interesting interpretation. What are we to make of the stories in the Bible? How do we determine their meaning and significance? Here are three things to pay attention to.

First, what is the *plot*? That is, what movement is there in the story? This could be physical, as in the case of the Israelites moving across the Sinai Peninsula in Exodus; it could be spiritual, as in the case of Samson in Judges; it could also be relational, as in Ruth; or political, as in 1 and 2 Kings. The question is, what development is there in the story? What is different at the end of the book, and why?

Another element to study is *characterization*. Who is in the cast of characters? How are they presented? What roles do they play? What decisions do they make? How do they relate to each other, and to God? What progress or regress do they make? Do they fail? If so, why? Why are they in the story? In what ways are they individuals, and in what ways are they representative of others? What do we like or dislike about them? What would we do in their place?

Here's a third issue to consider: In what ways is this story *true to life*? The stories of Scripture show us life as God wants us to see it. So we can ask: What questions does this story raise? What problems do the characters have to deal with? What lessons do they learn or not learn? What things do they encounter that we should be sure to avoid? Or how do they deal with things in life that are unavoidable? What do they discover about God?

There is much more to the narratives in Scripture. But if you start by asking yourself these kinds of questions, you'll go a long way toward understanding what the stories are all about.

Parables

Closely related to narrative are the parable and its cousin, the allegory. A parable is a brief tale that illustrates a moral principle. By far, most of the parables in Scripture come from the teaching of Jesus. In fact, we can infer from Matthew's account that the parable may have been His preferred method of communication (Matthew 13:34).

It's easy to see why. Parables are simple, memorable, and entertaining. Most are rather easy to understand. They deal with everyday matters such as farming, fishing, travel, money, and human relationships. And parables are usually intended to have a powerful impact. They jolt the listener into awareness by using basic ethical principles such as right and wrong (the sower and the three kinds of seed), love and compassion (the prodigal son, the good Samaritan), justice and mercy (the Pharisee and the tax collector).

It's worth noting that parables are a form of fiction. But that by no means implies that they do not convey truth. They communicate truth that cannot be communicated in any other way. A parable kind of sneaks up on people's blind sides, bypassing their defenses and appealing to their imagination and their hearts. It compels them to see some aspect of life in a completely new way. If you want to see a powerful example of that in action, read Nathan's parable about the poor man's sheep in 2 Samuel 12:1–10.

Poetry

The Bible contains some of the finest lines of verse ever composed. Indeed, some have become icons in our culture: "The Lord is my shepherd, I shall not want" (Ps. 23:1 NASB); "God is our refuge and strength, an ever-present help in trouble" (Ps. 46:1). The distinctive feature of poetry is its appeal to the emotions, as well as the imagination. That's why the psalms are so beloved. They express some of the deepest feelings, longings, rapture, and pain of the human heart.

But when you study biblical verse, make sure you understand the dynamics of Hebrew poetry. In the first place, most of the psalms were meant to be sung, not read. They were composed for worship, and many include prefatory notes on what kinds of instruments were to accompany them. So even though we no longer have the music to which they were sung, you should still listen for how they sound (which is true of all poetry).

One of the main features of Hebrew poetry is its extensive use of parallelism. If you look through the Book of Psalms, for instance, you'll notice that the majority of the verses have two lines. The two lines work off of each other to communicate meaning. (See "Background" to Psalms in the May reading.)

Another key to appreciating Hebrew poetry is to recognize hyperbole, which is extreme or exaggerated language that makes its point through overkill.

Here are some other interpretive questions to consider as you approach the poetry of the Bible: Who composed this material? Can you determine why? What is the central theme of the poem? What emotions does the verse convey, and what response does it produce? What questions does it ask? Which ones does it answer, and which does it leave unanswered? What does the poem say about God? About people? What images does the poet use to spark the imagination? Are there references to people, places, or events that you are unfamiliar with? If so, what can you find out about them elsewhere in Scripture or through secondary sources?

The Proverbs and Wisdom Literature

One of the richest quarries to mine in the biblical material is the broad category known as wisdom literature. In this genre, the writer assumes the role of a wizened veteran of life who is sharing his insights with a younger, less experienced, but teachable reader.

The book of Proverbs obviously belongs to this area. A proverb is a short, poignant nugget of truth, typically practical, and often concerned with the consequences of a course of behavior. Like the poetry of the psalms, proverbs make strategic use of parallelism, especially the pairing of opposites. For instance, Proverbs 15:27 says: "He who profits illicitly troubles his own house, but he who hates bribes will live" (NASB).

The Proverbs come right to the point. Of all the biblical material, they are perhaps the easiest to understand, though sometimes the hardest to apply. If you need a "spiritual vitamin" to perk up your way of life, chow down on the Proverbs. It will be a feast for your soul.

One word of caution, though—a proverb contains a principle, not a promise. A proverb tells you: this is how life basically works. What is left unsaid is the qualifier: Life does not always, 100 percent of the time, work this way.

Take Proverbs 21:17 (NASB) as a case in point: "He who loves pleasure will become a poor man; he who loves wine and oil will not become rich." The idea is that in the main, squandering one's time, energy, and resources on partying and living the easy life will eventually lead to poverty. Just think of the prodigal son. So if the goal is to grow one's wealth, a general principle for doing so is to apply oneself to honest labor and living a disciplined lifestyle.

Is the proverb guaranteeing that hard work and a disciplined lifestyle will lead to riches? No. Life doesn't work that way. There are too many other factors that contribute to the creation of wealth to say that hard work and discipline alone are all that it takes. Countless people in the world work very hard and keep impeccable personal habits, yet they have little to show for it, financially speaking. That does not negate the principle of the proverb. It merely shows that the principle is intended to point us in the right direction, not carry us all the way to our destination.

More problematic are the cases that appear to negate the proverb. Just as we know of hard workers who are not wealthy, we also know of people who spend their lives doing nothing but eating, drinking, and being merry, yet they happen to be quite rich. Indeed, some of them have gained their wealth by living a hedonistic lifestyle. Does that not contradict the truth of Proverbs 21:17? It certainly contradicts the warning of the author. But by doing so, it actually establishes the author's point, rather than defeat it. Sure, various factors (such as society's moral decline) may reward a given individual for pursuing nothing but pleasure. But that's an aberration, not the usual way of things. In the main, people who live solely for pleasure go broke. In the main, people who play with matches eventually get burned.

Note

1. C.S. Lewis, *A Preface to Paradise Lost* (London: Oxford Univ. Press, 1942), 1.

WHAT KIND OF LITERATURE IS THIS?: PART 2
PROPHECY AND APOCALYPTIC LITERATURE

The final, and perhaps most challenging, type of literature in the Bible is the prophetic. We tend to think of prophecy as a prediction for the future. And certainly the prophetic books look ahead. But a more striking feature is their tone of warning and judgment, and the use of a formula to denote direct words from God: "Thus saith the Lord!"

The role of the prophet in Scripture was not so much to tell the future, but to proclaim the words of the Lord; not to foretell, but to "forth-tell," as someone has well put it. God raised up prophets in Israel when it became clear that the people were determined to resist Him. The prophets' thankless task was to warn the nation of the dire consequences of continued disobedience, in hopes of sparking repentance and a return to the Lord.

In reading the prophets, it is critical that you re-create the situation. It is absolutely critical that you bombard the text with the six questions of selective Bible reading—who, what, where, when, why, and wherefore. Answering them will give you an invaluable database for considering these additional issues: What is the main problem that the prophet is addressing? What images does he use to describe it? What is the response of the people? What does this prophet's message tell you about God? What happens after this prophet delivers his message? Why do you think God included this book in His Word?

A special category of prophetic literature is called "apocalyptic," of which the book of Revelation is the primary example. As the term implies, apocalyptic literature deals with cataclysmic events of global proportions having to do with the end of the world. The language of apocalyptic is highly symbolic, and the events unfold in quick, dazzling displays of light, noise, and power.

This makes the genre fertile ground for speculation and subjective interpretation. To avoid that, I suggest that when you study Revelation, pay close attention to the structure of the book. What movement is there from the opening to the close? What changes come about? Also, who is the material written to? What was the historical and cultural context in which the writer was working? How might that have influenced his method of communication? In terms of understanding the book's symbols, look carefully at the Old Testament for insight into what the author is describing. Rather than worry about a time line for future events, ask what implications this book would have had for Christians in the early church.

The Names and Titles of Jesus

As we read the Gospels, we see that Jesus' own revelation about Himself was far from crystal clear. As in the teaching from His parables, Jesus did not "cast His pearls before swine," but gradually revealed Himself to that inner circle of disciples who had forsaken all to follow Him. The vocabulary of the synagogue allowed Him to speak of Himself by innuendo.

When we who are Christians use the word *Christ*, we read into it all we believe to be true of Jesus, including His deity. But in New Testament times, the Christ (from the Greek *christos*) or Messiah (from the Hebrew *mashiach*), though a special envoy from God, was not thought to be God Himself. As a descendant of the great king, He was known to be the "son of David." Because of Yahweh's special covenant with David, He was also referred to as the "son of God" (2 Samuel 7:14; 1 Chronicles 17:13). And because of the messianic understanding of Daniel 9 (especially vv. 13–14), another name for the Messiah was "the son of man," which elsewhere in the Hebrew Bible simply means "human being."

Jesus can be called the son of David, as He is a dozen times in the gospels, because He is a physical descendant of the king (Matthew 1; Luke 3). But although those who addressed Him as the son of David believed Him to be the Messiah, it was only after the resurrection that they knew Him to be *the* Son of David—like none they had expected.

Similarly, Jesus could make light of the title "son of God" in John 10:34–38 when dealing with a hostile audience, but those who saw through eyes of faith as He did His Father's work knew He was *the* Son of God like no other. And Jesus' own favorite label for Himself, "son of man," emphasized His true humanity while revealing Him as the Messiah to those believed in Him.

Jesus referred to Himself in one other unique and unexpected way. When Yahweh revealed Himself to Moses in Exodus 3:14, He proclaimed His name: "I AM WHO I AM." Of course, a normal human being could say, "I am," meaning "That's me," without claiming to be God. But when Jesus said, "Before Abraham was born, I am!" (John 8:58), His intentions were absolutely clear—that's why His audience attempted to stone Him on the spot. So whenever Jesus says, "I am," we can expect that to those with ears to hear, He means, "I am Yahweh."

THE MOODY HANDBOOK OF THEOLOGY

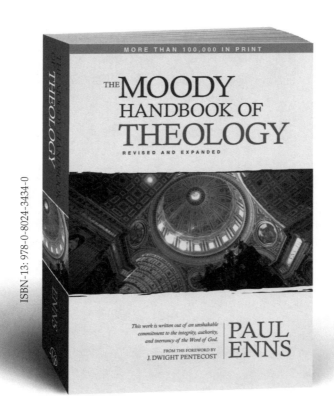

This book leads the reader into the appreciation and understanding of the essentials of Christian theology. It provides a concise doctrinal reference tool for newcomer and scholar and includes new material on the openness of God, health and wealth theology, the emergent church, rapture interpretations, feminism, and more.

MOODY
PUBLISHERS.

1-800-678-8812 · MOODYPUBLISHERS.COM

SEVEN REASONS WHY YOU CAN TRUST THE BIBLE

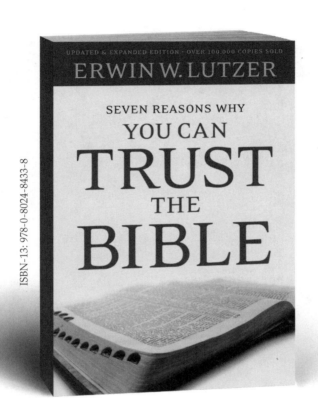

With the current cultural onslaught against the authority of God's Word, we explore the seven reasons why we can unequivocally trust and fully depend on the Bible. *Seven Reasons Why You Can Trust the Bible* is revised, expanded and includes Bible study questions at the end of each chapter. It is an effective resource for the lay Christian who desires to understand why we believe what we believe.

MOODY
PUBLISHERS.

1-800-678-8812 · MOODYPUBLISHERS.COM